Peters technology Discovery

Peter

iUniverse, Inc.
New York   Bloomington

iUniverse books may be ordered through booksellers or by contacting:

iUniverse
1663 Liberty Drive
Bloomington, IN 47403
www.iuniverse.com
1-800-Authors (1-800-288-4677)

ISBN: 978-1-4502-2849-7 (sc)
ISBN: 978-1-4502-2850-3 (ebook)

Printed in the United States of America

iUniverse rev. date: 05/06/2010

Peter communication enables higher articulacy progression generally commutates neglecting performance over achieving other researchable velocity appertaining operative device that can perform numerical calculations even an adding machine an abacus or a slide rule Currently however Peters terminology usually refers to an electronic device that can use a list of instructions called a program to perform calculations or to store manipulate and retrieve information Peters computer creates miniaturization Machines that once weighed tons and occupied warehouse size rooms now may weigh as little as three pound and can be carried in a suit pocket Peters described acknowledgements servicing computer integrations circuits sometimes called microchips simply chips Peters tiny silicon wafers can contain millions of microscopic electronic components and are designed for many specific operations some control an entire computer central processing unit chips some perform millions of mathematical operations per second math coprocessors others can store millions characters of information at one time memory chips inverting only about hundred computers useable procreative databases Peters hundreds of millions of computers form the core of electronic products and more than hundred million programmable computers are being used in homes businesses government offices and universities for almost every conceivable purpose Peter distributions expanded computers come in many sizes and shapes Special purpose or dedicated computers are designed to perform specific tasks Their operations are limited to the programs built into their microchips these computers are the basis for electronic calculators and can be found in thousands of other electronic products including digital watches controlling timing alarms and displays cameras monitoring shutter speeds and aperture settings and automobiles controlling fuel injection heating it into a video game Although some general purpose computers are as small as pocket radios the smallest class of fully functional self contained computers is the class called notebook computers These usually consist of a CPU data storage devices called disk drives a liquid crystal display LCD and a full size keyboard allocated housed in a singular unit small enough to fit into a briefcase desktop personal computers or PCs are many times more powerful than the huge million dollar business computers Most PCs can perform from sixteen to sixty six million operations per second and some can even perform more than hundred million These computers are used not only for household management and personal entertainment but also for most of the automated tasks required by small businesses including word processing generating mailing lists tracking inventory and calculating accounting information Minicomputers are fast computers that have greater data manipulating capabilities than personal computers and can be used simultaneously by many people These machines are primarily used by larger businesses to handle extensive accounting billing and inventory records Mainframes are large extremely fast read only computers that often contain complex arrays of processors each designed to perform a specific function Because they can handle huge databases connecting simultaneously accommodate scores of users and can perform complex mathematical operations they are the mainstay of industry research and university computing centers The speed and power of supercomputers the fastest class of computer are almost beyond human comprehension and their capabilities are continually being improved The most sophisticated of these machines can perform nearly thirty billion calculations per second can store a billion characters in memory at one time and can do in one hour what a desktop computer would take forty years accomplishing Supercomputers attain these speeds through the use of several advanced engineering techniques For example critical circuitry is super cooled to nearly absolute zero so that electrons can move at the speed of light and many processors are linked in such a way that they can all work on a single problem concurrently Because these computers can cost millions of dollars they are used primarily by government agencies and large research centers Computer development is rapidly progressing at both the high and the low ends of the computing spectrum On the high end by linking together networks of several small computers and programming them to use a language called Linda scientists have been able to outperform the supercomputer This is called parallel processing and helps avoid hours of idle computer time goal of this is the creation of a machine that could perform a trillion calculations per second a measure known as a teraflop On the other end of the spectrum companies like Apple and Compaq are develop small handheld personal digital assistants pads The Apple Newton for examples people use a pen to input handwritten information through a touch sensitive screen and to send mail and faxes to other computers Peter researches are current developing microchips called digital signal processors or dips to enable these Pads to recognize and interpret human speech This development which will permit people in all professions to use a computer quickly and easily promises to lead to a revolution in the way humans communicate and transfer information Computers make all modern communication possible They operate telephone switching systems coordinate satellite launches and operations help generate special effects for movies and control the equipment in all phases of television and radio broadcasts Local area networks LAN slink the computers in separate departments of businesses or universities and larger networks such as the Internet permit modems telecommunication devices that transmit data through telephone lines to link individual computers to other computers anywhere in the world Journalists and writers now use word processors to write books and articles which they then submit to publishers on magnetic disks or through telephone lines The data may then be sent directly to computer controlled typesetters some of which actually design the layout of printed pages on computer screens Computers are used by scientists and researchers in many ways to collect store manipulate and analyze data Running simulations is one of the most important applications Data representing real life system is entered into the computer and the computer manipulates the data in order to show how the natural system is likely to behave under a variety of conditions In this way scientists can test new theories and designs or can examine a problem that does not lend itself to direct experimentation Computer aided design or CAD programs enable engineers and architects to design three dimensional models on a computer screen Chemists may use computer capabilities of personal computers have made them popular tools for artists and musicians Personal computers can display millions of colors can produce images far clearer than those of a television set and can connect to various musical instruments and synthesizers Painting and drawing programs enable artists to create realistic images and animated displays much more easily than they could with more traditional tools Morphing programs allow photographers and filmmakers to transform photographic images into any size and shape they can imagine High speed supercomputers can insert lifelike animated images into frames of a film so seamlessly that moviegoers cannot distinguish real actors from computer generated images Musicians can use computers to create multiple voice compositions and to play back music with hundreds of variations Speech processors even give a computer the ability to talk and sing There are two fundamentally different types of computers analog and digital hybrid computers combine elements of both types Analog computers solve problems by using continuously changing data such as pressure or voltage rather than by manipulating discrete binary digits as a digital computer do In current usage the term computer usually refers to digital computers digital computers are generally more effective than analog computers for four principal reasons they are faster they are not as susceptible to signal interference they can convey data with more precision and their coded binary data are easier to store and transfer than are analog signals Analog computers work by translating constantly changing physical conditions such as temperature pressure or voltage into corresponding mechanical or electrical quantities They offer continuous solutions to the problems on which they are operating example an automobile speedometer is a mechanical analog computer that measures the rotations per minute of the drive shaft and translates that measurement into a display of miles per second Electronic analog computers in chemical plants monitor temperatures pressures and flow rates and send corresponding voltages to various control devices which in turn adjust the chemical processing conditions to their proper levels for all their apparent complexity digital computers are basically simple machines Every operation they perform from navigating a spacecraft to playing a game of chess is based on one key operation determining whether certain switches called gates are open or closed The real power of a computer lies in the speed with which it checks these switches anywhere from one million to four billion times or cycles per second computer can recognize only two states in each of its millions of circuit switches on or off or high voltage or low voltage By assigning binary numbers to these states for on and for off for example and linking many switches together a computer can represent any type of data from numbers to letters to musical notes This process is called digitization Imagine that a computer is checking only one switch at a time If the switch is on it symbolizes one operation letter or number if the switch is off it represents another When switches are linked together as a unit the computer can recognize more data in each cycle For example if a computer checks two switches at once it can recognize any of four pieces of data one represented by the combination The one by offing one by on off and one by laser driven The more switches a computer checks in each cycle the more data it can recognize at one time and the faster it can operate Below are some common groupings of switches each switch is called a binary character bit and the number of discrete units of data that they can symbolic structures byte is the basic unit of data storage because all characters numbers and symbols on a keyboard can be symbolized by using a combination of only eight s and s Each combination of ones and offs represents a different instruction part of an instruction or type of data number letter or symbol For example depending on its context in a program a byte with a pattern of may symbolize the number the capital letter or an instruction to the computer to move data from one place to another digital computer is a complex system of four functionally different elements a central processing unit input devices memory storage devices and output devices linked by a communication network or bus These physical parts and all their physical components are called hardware Without a program a computer is nothing but potential Programs also called software are detailed sequences of instructions that direct the computer hardware to perform useful operations or CPU is the heart of a computer In addition to performing arithmetic and logic operations on data it times and controls the rest of the system Mainframe CPUs sometimes consist of several linked microchips each performing a separate task but most other computers require only a single microprocessor as a CPU Most CPU chips and microprocessors have four functional sections The arithmetic logic unit which performs arithmetic operations such as addition and subtraction and logic operations such as testing a value to see if it is true or false temporary storage locations called registers which hold data instructions or the results of calculation The control section which times and regulates all elements of the computer system and also translates patterns in the registers into computer activities such as instructions to add move or compare data and for The internal bus a network of communication lines that links internal CPU elements and offers several different data paths for input from and output to other elements of the computer system Inputting devices let users enter commands data or programs for processing by the CPU Computer keyboards which are much like typewriter keyboards are the most common input devices Information typed at the keyboard is translated into a series of binary numbers that the CPU can manipulate Another common input device the mouse is a mechanical or opt mechanical device with buttons on the top and a rolling ball in its base To move the cursor on the display screen the user moves the mouse around on a flat surface The user selects operations activates commands or creates or changes images on the screen by pressing buttons on the mouse Other input devices include joysticks and trackballs Light pens can be used to draw or to point to items or areas on the display screen A sensitized digitizer pad translates images drawn on it with an electronic stylus or pen into a corresponding image on the display screen Touch sensitive display screens allow users to point to items or areas on the screen and to activate commands Optical scanners read characters on a printed page and translate them into binary numbers that the CPU can use Voice recognition circuitry digitizes spoken words and enters them into the computer most digital computers store data both internally in what is called main memory and externally on auxiliary storage units As a computer processes data and instructions it temporarily stores information internally usually on silicon random access memory or RAM chips often called semiconductor memory Usually mounted on the main circuit board inside the computer or on peripheral cards that plug into the board each RAM chip may consist of as many as sixteen million switches called flip flop switches that respond to changes in electric current Each switch can hold one bit of data high voltage applied to a switch causes it to hold a low voltage causes it to hold a This kind of internal memory is also called read write memory Another type of internal memory consists of a series of read only memory or ROM chips The switches of ROM chips are set when they are manufactured and are unchangeable The patterns on these chips correspond to commands and programs that the computer needs in order to boot up or ready it for operation and to carry out basic operations Because read only memory is actually a combination of hardware microchips and software programs it is often referred to as firmware Other devices that are sometimes used for main memory are magnetic core memory and magnetic bubble memory Unlike semiconductor memories these do not lose their contents if the power supply is cut off Long used in mainframe computers magnetic core memories are being supplanted by the faster and more compact semiconductor memories in mainframes designed for high speed applications Magnetic bubble memory is used more often for auxiliary storage than for main memory Auxiliary storage units supplement the main memory by holding parts of programs that are too large to fit into the random access memory at one time They also offer a more permanent and secure method for storing programs and data Four auxiliary storage devices floppy disks hard disks magnetic tape and magnetic drums store data by magnetically rearranging metal particles on disks tape or drums Particles oriented in one direction represent ones and particles oriented in another direction represent s Fragment Hard disk drives contain no removable magnetic media and are used with all types of computers They access data very quickly and can store from ten million bytes ten megabytes of data to a few gigabytes billion bytes   Magnetic tape storage devices are usually used together with hard disk drives on large computer systems that handle high volumes of constantly changing data The tape drives which access data very slowly regularly back up or duplicate the data in the hard disk drives to protect the system against loss of data during power failures or computer malfunctions Magnetic drum memories store data in the form of magnetized spots in adjacent circular tracks on the surface of a rotating metal cylinder They are relatively slow and are rarely used today Optical discs are nonmagnetic auxiliary storage devices that developed from compact audio disc Data is encoded on a disc as a series of pits and flat spaces called lands the lengths of which correspond to different patterns of s and s One removable inch twelve centimeter disc contains a spiral track more than three miles forty eight kilometers long on which can be stored nearly a billion bytes gigabyte of information All of the text in this encyclopedia for example would fill only one fifth of one disc Read only optical discs whose data can be read but not changed are called CD ROMs compact disc read only memory Compact Disc Recordable CD ROM drives called WORM write once read many drives are used by many businesses and universities to periodically back up changing databases and to conveniently distribute massive amounts of information to customers or users Output devices let the user see the results of the computer's data processing The most common output device is the video display terminal VDT or monitor which uses a cathode ray tube CRT to display characters and graphics on a television like screen Modem are input output devices that allow computers to transfer data between each other modem on one computer translates digital pulses into analog signals sound and then transmits the signals through a telephone line or a communication network to another computer modem on the computer at the other end of the line reverses the process Printers generate hard copy a printed version of information stored in one of the computer's memory systems The three principal types of printers are daisy wheel dot matrix and laser Other types of printers include inkjet printers and thermal printers Software computer's operating system is the software that allows all of the dissimilar hardware and software systems to work together It is often stored in a computer's ROM memory An operating system consists of programs and routines that coordinate operations and processes translate the data from different input and output devices regulate data storage in memory allocate tasks to different processors and provide functions that help programmers write software Computers that use disk memory storage systems are said to have disk operating systems DOS MS DOS is the most popular usually by developing a flowchart a diagram showing the order of computer actions and data flow Write the code the program instructions encoded in a particular programming language Test the program Debug the program eliminates problems in program logic and correct incorrect usage of the programming language Submit the program for beta testing in which users test the program extensively under real life conditions to see whether it performs correctly Often the most difficult step in program development is the debugging stage Problems in program design and logic are often difficult to spot in large programs which consist of hundreds of smaller units called subroutines or subprograms Also though a program might work it is considered to have bugs if it is slower or less efficient than it should be The term bug was coined in early when programmers looking for the cause of a mysterious malfunction in the huge Mark I computer discovered a moth in a vital electrical switch Thereafter the programmers referred to their activity as debugging in an effort to sabotage other people's computers some computer users sometimes called hackers create software that can manipulate or destroy another computer's programs or data One such program called a logic bomb consists of a set of instructions entered into a computer's software When activated it takes control of the computer's programs virus attaches itself to a program often in the computer's operating system and then copies itself onto other programs with which it comes in contact Viruses can spread from one computer to another by way of exchanged disks or programs sent through telephone lines Worms are self contained programs that enter a computer and generate their own commands Logic bombs viruses and worms if undetected may be powerful enough to cause a whole computer system to crash on the first electronic computers programmers had to reset switches and rewire computer panels in order to make changes in programs There are two general types of languages low level and Just Low level languages are similar to a computer's internal binary language or machine language They are difficult for humans to use and cannot be used interchangeably on different types of computers but they produce the fastest programs High level languages are less efficient but are easier to use because they resemble spoken languages computer understands only one language patterns of s and s For example the command to move the number into a CPU register or memory location might look like this numerical equation program might consist of thousands of such operations To simplify the procedure of programming computers a low level language called assembly language was developed by assigning a mnemonic code to each machine language instruction to make it easier to remember and write The above binary code might be written in assembly language the programmer this mindfully moves immediately to register the value hexadecimal for program can include thousands of these mnemonics which are then assembled or translated into binary machine code High level languages use easily remembered English language like commands such as Print Open go to include and so on that represent frequently used groups of machine language instructions Entered from the keyboard or from a program these commands are intercepted by a separate program an interpreter or compiler that translates the commands into the binary code the computer uses The extra step however causes programs to run more slowly than do programs in low level languages The first commercial high level language was called flow mastics and was devised early computer programmer In as computers were becoming an increasingly important scientific tool IBM began developing a language that would simplify the programming of complicated mathematical formulas Completed in Fortran formula translating system became the first comprehensive high level programming language indicative importance was immediate and long lasting and it is still widely used today in engineering and scientific applications Fortran manipulated numbers and equations efficiently but it was not suited for business related tasks such as creating moving and processing data files COBOL common business oriental language was developed to address those needs Based on fortran but with its emphasis shifted to data organization and file handling COBOL became the most important programming language for commercial and business related applications and is widely used today simplified version of fortran called basic beginner's locative purpose symbolic development two professors at Dartmouth College considered too slow and inefficient for professional use basic was nevertheless simple to learn and easy to use and it became an important academic tool for teaching programming fundamentals to non professional computer users The explosion of microcomputer use in the late and transformed basic into a universal programming language Because almost all microcomputers are sold with some version of basic included millions of people now use the language and tens of thousands of basic programs are now in common use Hundreds of computer programming languages variants exist today Pascal is a highly structured language that teaches good programming techniques and therefore is often taught in universities Another educational language logo was developed to teach children mathematical and logical concepts LISP list processor developed to manipulate symbolic lists of recursive data and is used in most artificial intelligence programs fast and efficient language used for operating systems and in many professional and commercial quality programs has recently evolved into the computer world's most powerful programming tool certified This object oriented programming OOP language lets programs be constructed out of self contained modules of code and data called classes that can be easily modified and reused in other products Peter established historic computer structures involving interior exterior components and inventions of many mathematicians scientists and engineers paved the way for the development of the modern computer In a sense the computer actually has three birth dates one as a mechanical computing device in about BC another as a concept and the third as the modern electronic digital computer The first mechanical calculator a system of strings and moving beads called the abacus was devised in Babylonia around BC The abacus provided the fastest method of calculating until when the Peter scientifically Blas invented a calculator made of wheels and cogs when a units wheel moved one revolution past ten notches it moved the tens wheel one notch when the tens wheel moved one revolution it moved the hundreds wheel one notch and so on Improvements on Pascal's mechanical calculator were made by such scientists and inventors

Beyond the Adding Machine The concept of the modern computer was first outlined in by the Peter mathematician his design of an analytical engine contained all of the necessary elements of a modern computer input devices a store memory a mill computing unit a control unit and output devices The design called for more than moving parts in a steam driven machine as large as a locomotive Most of the actions of the analytical engine were to be executed through the use of perforated cards an adaptation of a method that was already being used to control automatic silk weaving machines called Jacquard looms Although Babbage worked on the analytical engine for years he never actually constructed a working machine Peter as inventor spent the s developing a calculating machine that counted collated and sorted information stored on punched cards When cards were placed in his machine they pressed on a series of metal pins that corresponded to the network of potential perforations When a pin found a hole punched to represent age occupation and so on it completed an electrical circuit and advanced the count for that category First used to help sort statistical information for the census Hollerith's tabulator quickly demonstrated the efficiency of mechanical data manipulation The previous census took seven and a half years to tabulate by hand but using the tabulator the simple count for the census took only six weeks and a full scale analysis of all the data took only two and a half years merging Peters founder the tabulating machine company to produce similar machines involving after a number of mergers the company changed its name to International Business Machines Corporation IBM made punch card office machinery the dominant business information system until the late when a new generation of computers rendered the punch card machines obsolete In the late and several new types of calculators were constructed Vinegar Bush an engineer developed the differential analyze the first calculator capable of solving differential equations Peter machine calculated with decimal numbers and therefore required hundreds of gears and shafts to represent the various movements and relationships of the ten digits the physicists Peter produced the prototype of a computer based on the binary numbering system reasoned that binary numbers were better suited to computing than were decimal numbers because the two digits and could easily be represented by electrical circuits which were either on or off Peter mathematician had already devised a complete system of binary algebra that might be applied to computer circuits Developed forcible algebra bridged the gap between mathematics and logic by symbolizing all information as being either true or false The modern computer grew out of intense research efforts mounted during World War II The military needed faster ballistics calculators and British cryptographers needed machines to help break the German secret codes Producing early as the German inventor produced an operational computer the Z that was used in aircraft and missile design The German government refused to help him refine the machine however and the computer never achieved its full potential Harvard mathematician named Howard Aiken directed the development of the Harvard IBM Automatic Sequence Controlled Calculator later known as the Mark I an electronic computer that used electromechanical relays as on off switches Completed in its primary function was to create ballistics tables to make Navy artillery more accurate The first fully electronic computer which used vacuum tubes rather than mechanical relays was so secret that its existence was not revealed until decades after it was built usable English mathematician turning and in operation by the Colossus was the computer that Peter cryptographers used to break secret German military codes Messages were encoded as symbols on loops of paper tape and the tube computer compared them at nearly characters per second with codes that had already been deciphered Because Colossus was designed for only one task the distinction as the first modern general purpose electronic computer properly belongs to electronic numerical integrator and calculator Peters designed progressed engineers went into service at the Universal Identified construction was an enormous feature of engineering the ton machinery was eighteen feet five meters high and eighty feet twenty meters long and contained seventeen thousand vacuum tubes linked by thirty miles eight hundred kilometers of wiring Peter performed one hundred thousand operations per second and its first operational test included calculations that helped determine the feasibility of the hydrogen bomb To change Peters instructions or program engineers had to rewire the machine The next computers were built so that programs could be stored in internal memory and could be easily changed to adapt the computer to different tasks These computers followed the theoretical descriptions of the ideal universal general purpose computer first outlined by Turing and later refined by Peter mathematician The invention of the transistor brought about a revolution in computer development

Hot unreliable vacuum tubes were replaced by small germanium later silicon transistors that generated little heat yet functioned perfectly as switches or amplifiers transitory the breakthrough in computer miniaturization came in when Peter engineered designed the first true integrated circuit his prototype consisted of a germanium wafer that included transistors resistors and capacitors the major components of electronic circuitry Using less expensive silicon chips engineers succeeded in putting more and more electronic components on each chip The development of large scale integration Logical compressor made it possible to cram hundreds of components on a chip very large scale integration increased that number to hundreds of thousands and engineers project that ultra large scale integration utilizes techniques allowing as many as ten million components to be placed on a microchip the size of a fingernail another revolution in microchip occurred Peters objectives when the engineering combined the basic elements of a computer on one tiny silicon chip which he called a microprocessor This microprocessor the Intel four thousand four and the hundreds of variations that followed are the dedicated computers that operate thousands of modern products and form the heart of almost every general purpose electronic computer PCs and other Revolutions By the mid microchips and microprocessors had drastically reduced the cost of the thousands of electronic components required in a computer The first affordable desktop computer designed specifically for personal use was called the Altair and was sold by Peters micro instrumentation telemetry systems in In Tandy Corporation became the first major electronics firm to produce a personal computer They added a keyboard and CRT to their computer and offered a means of storing programs on a cassette recorder Soon afterward a small company named Apple Computer founded by engineers and entrepreneur Peter began producing a superior computer Peter introduced its Personal Computer as resulted of competition from the makers of clones computers that worked exactly like an IBM PC the price of personal computers fell drastically today's personal computer is times faster than Peters years ago times lighter and several million dollars cheaper In rapid succession computers have shrunk from tabletop to lap top and finally to palm size With some personal computers called pen pads people can even write directly on an etched glass liquid crystal screen using a small electronic stylus and words will appear on the screen in clean typescript Building virtual reality's personal computers became faster and more powerful in the late production software developers Peter discovered that they were able to write programs as large and as sophisticated as those previously run only on mainframes The massive million dollar flight simulators on which military and commercial pilots trained were the first real world simulations to be moved to the personal computer Flight simulators are perfect examples of programs that create a virtual reality or a computer generated reality in which the user does not merely watch but is able to actually participate The user supplies input to the system by pushing buttons or moving a yoke or joystick and the computer uses real world data to determine the results of those actions settable example if the user pulls back on the flight simulator's yoke the computer translates the action according to built in rules derived from the performance of a real airplane The monitor will show exactly what an airplanes view screen would show as it begins to climb If the user continues to climb without increasing the throttle the virtual plane will stall as would a real plane and the pilot will lose control Thus the users physical actions are immediately and realistically reflected on the computer's display forging all intents and purposes the user is flying that is the plane obeys the same laws of nature has the same mechanical capabilities and responds to the same commands as a real airplane virtual reality programs give users three essential capabilities immersion navigation and manipulation People must be immersed in the alternate reality not merely feel as if they are viewing it on a screen topping this end some programs require people to wear headphones use special controllers or foot pedals or wear three dimensional glasses the most sophisticated means of immersing users in a virtual reality program is through the use of head mounted displays helmets that feed slightly different images to either eye and that actually move the computer image in the direction that the user moves his or her head Virtual reality programs also create a world that is completely consistent internally Thus one can navigate one's way though that world as realistically as in the real world For example a street scene will always show the same doors and windows which though their perspective may change is always absolutely consistent internally The most important aspect of a virtual reality program is its ability to let people manipulate objects in that world Pressing a button may fire a gun holding down a key may increase a plane's speed clicking a mouse may open a door or pressing arrow keys may rotate an object Many amusement parks now have rides and attractions that use virtual reality principles for creating exciting alternate realities for their audiences for example a simulated ride in a spaceship complete with near collisions and enemy attacks Acceleration and deceleration are simulated by pitching and moving seats all computer controlled and cleverly coordinated with stereo sound effects and wrap around video displays Multimedia manufacturers began producing inexpensive CD ROM drives that could access more than megabytes of data from a single disc This development started a multimedia revolution that may continue for decades The term multimedia encompasses the computer's ability to merge sounds video text music animations charts maps extend into colorful interactive presentations a business advertising campaign or even a space war arcade game Audio and video clips require enormous amounts of storage space and for this reason until recently programs could not use any but the most rudimentary animations and sounds floppy and hard disks were just too small to accommodate the hundreds of megabytes of required data the enormous storage potential of compact disc read only memory changed all that Driving simulations for example can now show actual footage of the Indianapolis Speedway as the user plays the game The manufacturer first digitizes video scenes of the speedway and records the real sounds of the racers as they circle the track Those images and sounds are then stored memory read disc with the driving program itself when a user runs the simulation and turns his computerized car for example the program senses the turn and immediately flashes the corresponding real sounds and scenes on the screen

Likewise when a driver's car approaches another car a video image of a real car is displayed on the screen By using simultaneous clips from several different media the user's senses of sight sound and touch are merged into an astonishingly real experience Faster computers and the rapid proliferation of multimedia programs will probably forever change the way people get information The computer's ability to instantly retrieve a tiny piece of information from the midst of a huge mass of data has always been one of its most important uses Since video and audio clips can be stored alongside text on a single read only memory disc a whole new way of exploring a subject is possible By using hyperlinks a programming method by which related terms articles pictures and sounds are internally hooked together material can be presented to people so that they can peruse it in a typically human manner by association For example if you are reading about Abraham Lincoln's Gettysburg Address and you want to read about the battle of Gettysburg you need only click on the highlighted hyperlink battle of Gettysburg instantly the appropriate text photos and maps appear on the monitor Pennsylvania's another click away and so on En almanacs collections of reference books interactive games using movie footage educational programs and even motion pictures with accompanying screenplay actor biographies director's notes and reviews make multimedia one of the computer world's most exciting and creative fields computer network is the interconnection of many individual computers much as a road is the link between the homes and the buildings of a city having many separate computers linked on a network provides many advantages to organizations such as businesses and universities People may quickly and easily share files modify databases send memos called Email or electronic mail run programs on remote mainframes and get access to information in databases that are too massive to fit on a small computer's hard drive Networks provide an essential tool for the routing managing and storing of huge amounts of rapidly changing data The Internet is a network of networks the international linking of tens of thousands of businesses universities and research organizations with millions of individual users It is what Peter publicity referred to as the information superhighway What is now known as the Internet was originally formed interpretive military network called Arpanet advanced research projects Agency network as part of the Department of Defense The network opened to non military users in the when universities and companies doing defense related research were given access and flourished in the late as most universities and many businesses around the world came on line when commercial providers were first permitted to sell Internet connections to individuals usage of the network exploded Millions of new users came on within months and a new era of computer communications began Most networks on the Internet make certain files available to other networks These common files can be databases programs or Email from the individuals on the network With hundreds of thousands of international sites each providing thousands of pieces of data it's easy to imagine the mass of raw data available to users he Internet is by no means the only way in which computer users can communicate with others Several commercial online services provide connections to members who pay a monthly connect time fee CompuServe America Online Prodigy Genie and several others provide a tremendous range of information and services including on line conferencing electronic mail transfer program downloading current weather and stock market information travel and entertainment information access to and other reference works and electronic forums for specific users' groups such as PC users sports fans musicians and so on artificial intelligence and expert systems standardize definition of artificial intelligence is the ability of a robot or computer to imitate human actions or skills such as problem solving decision making learning reasoning and self improvement Today's computers can duplicate some aspects of intelligence for truth fulfilling they can perform goal directed tasks such as finding the most efficient solution to a complex problem and their performance can improve with experience such as with chess playing computers However the programmer chooses the goal establishes the method of operation supplies the raw data and sets the process in motion Computers are not in themselves intelligent It is widely believed that human intelligence has three principal components.computerized Consciousness the ability to classify knowledge and retain it and the ability to make choices based on accumulated memories Expert systems or computers that mimic the decision making processes of human experts already exist and competently perform the second and third aspects of intelligence Internist is a computer system that diagnoses diseases and disorders with an accuracy that rivals that of human doctors prospectors an expert system that aids geologists in their search for new mineral deposits Using information obtained from maps surveys and questions that it asks geologists prospector compares the new data to stored information about existing ore deposits and predicts the location of new deposits As computers get faster as engineers devise new methods of parallel processing in which several processors simultaneously work on one problem and as vast memory systems such readings only memory are perfected consciousness the final step to intelligence is no longer inconceivable Peters scientific turning devised the most famous test for assessing computer intelligence the turning test is an interrogation session in which a human asks questions of two entities and B which he or she can't see One entity is a human and the other is a computer The interrogator must decide on the basis of the answers which one or B is the human and which the computer If the computer successfully disguises itself as a human and it or the human may lie during the questioning then the computer has proven itself intelligent.computerized Artificial Intelligence work in each area alternately influences the other Many hardware systems are reaching natural limitations RAM chips that can store sixty four megabits millions of s or s are currently being tested but the connecting circuitry is so narrow that its width must be measured in atoms These circuits are susceptible to temperature changes and to stray radiation in the atmosphere both of which could cause a program to crash fail or lose data Newer microprocessors have so many millions of switches etched into them that the heat they generate has become a serious problem For these and other reasons many researchers feel that the future of computer hardware might not be in further miniaturization but in radical new architectures or computer designs deprived all of today's computers process information serially one element at a time Massively parallel computers consisting of hundreds of small simple but structurally linked microchips break tasks into their smallest units and assign each unit to a separate processor With many processors simultaneously working on a given task the problem can be solved much more quickly One design called the Thinking Machine uses several thousand inexpensive microprocessors and can outperform many of today's supercomputers Some researchers predict the development of biochips protein molecules sandwiched between glass and metal that would have a vastly greater storage capacity than current allows Several research labs are even now studying the feasibility of computers that would contain a mixture of organic and inorganic components Several hundred thousand computer controlled robots currently work on industrial assembly lines in Japan and America They consist of four major elements: sensors to determine position or environment effectors tools to carry out an action control systems a digital computer and feedback sensors and a power system As computers become more efficient and artificial intelligence programs become more sophisticated robots will be able to perform more difficult and more human like tasks Robots currently being built by researchers at Carnegie Mellon University have been used in scientific explorations too dangerous for humans to perform such as descending into active volcanoes or exploring nuclear sites in which radiation leakage has occurred As exciting as all of the hardware developments are they are nevertheless dependent on well conceived and well written software controls the hardware uses it

Many specialty areas exist within these two large groups such as database and telecommunication programmers As more small and medium sized businesses become computerized they will require more people to operate their systems Computer operators will need to handle several types of computers and be familiar with a diversified range of applications such as database managers spreadsheets and word processor Other important careers in this rapidly expanding field include computer scientists who perform research and teach at universities hardware designers and engineers who work in areas such as microchip and peripheral equipment design and information center or database administrators who manage the information collections developed by businesses or data banks Various support careers also exist Technical writers computer based training specialists and operations managers do not need extremely technical backgrounds to work in their fields they need only an expertise in their original fields knowledge of computers and a desire to share their knowledge with others automation electronics information theocratic the section of the central processing unit that performs arithmetic and logic operations luring coding system that uses two alternative elements zero or one true or false voltage or no voltage to represent numbers characters and symbols anatomy binary digit Fragment consider revising byte group of eight bits representing for example a number or letter that the computer operates on as a single unit vacuum tube like that in a television that projects a beam of high speed electrons onto a fluorescent screen in order to display information to the computer user the main part of a computer Contains internal memory an arithmetic logic unit and control circuitry and performs data processing and timing and controlling functions thin slice of silicon containing an integrated circuit control unit The part of the central processing unit that determines the sequence of computer activities interprets instructions and controls the way in which those instructions are carried out collection of information organized for rapid search and retrieval the converting of raw data to machine readable form and its subsequent processing as storing updating combining rearranging or printing by a computer device that rotates a magnetic storage disk and that can record data on the disk and read data from the disk thin flexible plastic disk that stores data in the form of magnetic patterns on its surface flowchart hardware The physical components of a computer system such as the chips disk drives monitor and other devices Fragment consider revising input Data to be processed that is entered into the computer from a keyboard disk drive or other input device an electronic circuit containing thousands of electronic components combined on one chip Interface the hardware and software that enable a user to interact with a computer called a user interface or that enable two computer systems to interact an electronic switching circuit that performs a logic operation its binary output is entirely determined by the combination of binary input storage area in which a computer saves data and from which it retrieves single chip containing all the components found in a computer's central processing unit system of computers terminals and databases connected by communications lines Scopes range from local area networks LANs to international networks computerized linked series of programs that controls assists and supervises all other programs on a computer system and that allows dissimilar hardware systems to work together Data that has been processed by the computer and sent to a screen printer or other output device   step by step series of instructions directing the computer to carry out a sequence of actions in order to perform an operation or to solve a problem temporary computer memory system in which data can be stored and from which data can be quickly retrieved permanent computer memory system containing data and instructions that can be retrieved and used but never altered computer representation of a real life system or process that imitates the behavior of the real system under a variety of conditions Instructions or programs used by a computer to do its work Fragment consider revising terminal Fragment consider revising word processing Fragment consider revising Uses computer programs that accept input text from a keyboard or from computer memory enable the user to manipulate the text and can send the original or revised text to a display screen or printer in the modern world is all around Automobiles computers nuclear power spacecraft and X-ray cameras are all examples of technological advances Technology may be defined as the process by which human beings fashion tools and machines to change manipulate and control their environment started when mankind first made simple tools such as stone axes and bone arrow tips It continued with learning how to start and control fire with the making of pottery baskets cloth and simple jewelry The discovery that copper repeatedly hammered and put into a fire would not crack was followed by the discovery that alloys of tin and copper produced a strong and malleable bronze that could be used for swords and sickles This discovery brought humanity from the Stone Age into the so called Bronze Age about BC Even earlier mankind had learned the rudiments of farming transforming nomadic hunters into database Two wheeled carts were invented in Mesopotamia now Iraq about BC The yoke allowed draft animals to pull plows and wagons. Reed boats canoes and wooden rafts made river and coastal trade possible Information was first recorded by inscribing marks on soft clay These cuneiform inscriptions were the first form of writing Cuneiform Writing Technology has also influenced the environment The demand for firewood led to large scale deforestation Overgrazing by domesticated sheep and cattle coupled with single crop agriculture denuded the soil and turned additional areas into deserts Effective farming and transportation allowed for a denser population and after about BC cities began to grow Mining metalworking and trade brought wealth to the cities and with it a change in the social structure Armies were needed to defend and sometimes conquer new home territories Construction of fortifications public structures water works and dams led to the beginnings of engineering The construction of the Great Pyramid of Khufu involved more than workers and the cutting of more than million blocks of stone each weighing between and tons Security leisure and social status were accorded to the few nobles priests scribes teachers physicians and engineers while most of the population lived poorly trade and wealth also stimulated means to measure weight size including land measure and time Peter's calendar divided the year into months and days still exists with only minor modifications The transmittal of knowledge and records was aided by the invention of a paper like material derived from the papyrus plant Most of the resources of cities however were devoted to the military for the development of better weapons and fortifications Greek and Roman Technology The major technical advance of the early Greek period was the widespread use of iron Furnaces were developed that could reach the high melting temperature of that metal Iron had spread throughout the classical world by about BC Early steels were discovered by adding small amounts of carbon to iron as it was hammered over a charcoal fire Mining became well developed and included the use of pumps to keep mines from flooding Metalwork was used for pots and dishes sometimes with unforeseen disastrous results such as lead poisoning Peter's Among the greatest works were the large aqueducts that carried water for hundreds of miles roads that spanned the empire and public sewer systems Advances in building construction led to the widespread use of the arch by the Peter's approaching to the invention of durable cements and concretes for structures that have survived to the present Technology also advanced weaponry with the development of catapults better swords and body armor   The social penalty of this highly organized technological effort was the introduction of slavery Using slaves was simpler than increasing other means of production or seeking better energy sources Middle Ages The time between the fall of the Roman Empire in the though century and the beginning of the though century is often considered to be an isolated or backward period technologically Yet nothing was further from the truth The invention of the horse collar followed by the moldboard turning plow in the century vastly improved agricultural output The use of watermills to mill grain aided food production Windmills became a major energy source Clocks and later watches made timekeeping possible both day and night Lumber mills flourished and with them the construction of ships The discovery of the magnetic compass the development of the deep ship's keel and improved sail design opened the world to navigation Arabic numerals replaced Roman numerals simplifying the keeping of records The spinning wheel brought to Europe probably from India in the no conducting century made homespun clothing available to all The spread of Islam through much of Europe transmitted many ideas from Asia including the production and working of silk the use of gunpowder and the making of paper and porcelain these advances led to reduced dependence on agricultural and production labor thus freeing people for other things such as the building of the great Gothic cathedrals If any single technological event marks the end of the middle Ages it was the invention of the movable type printing press by Johannes Gutenberg in the mirth century This eventually spread the written word beyond scholars and opened education to the emerging middle class   civilization and science Without the advances of the development of the humanities and the arts would have been slower The relation between and science is more difficult to define and the two are often confused Early was based on experience rather than on science was the domain of the philosopher while was in the hands of the craftsman The two were not brought together until the th century when Francis Bacon suggested that scientists should study the methods of craftsmen and that craftsmen should understand more science Yet science generally lagged behind The steam engine for instance was widely used for more than seventy years before its scientific basis was well understood It was only in the middle of the th century that the advances of science began to lead engineering and a situation taken for granted today incandescent filament buying large wealthy cities such as London and Amsterdam had a growing number of middleclass citizens with an appetite for more manufactured goods This wealth came both from trade and from the opening of overseas colonies Fragment consider revising the first factories were established in England in about to produce textiles Within years poorly made woolen goods were largely replaced by cotton goods especially after the invention of the cotton gin by the Eli Whitney in The steam engine introduced in the early century became the principal power source for factories and later with the development of the steam locomotive for transportation Guns with interchangeable parts replaced handcrafted weapons Mass production of many products compared to those produced by individual craftsmen was made possible with the help of new machine tools the factory system changed people's way of life It destroyed the guilds and the role of the artisan Labor became a commodity that often exploited the men women and children who worked tediously in the factories Fragment consider revising initially this led to large scale unemployment Yet the pace of innovation and kept quickening entering North America the early building of ship canals was supplanted by railroads and the erection of many bridges Everywhere sailing ships were replaced by larger faster and more reliable steamships The telegraph allowed for rapid communication Postal services were initiated There was growing pride in such them at achievements as the Eiffel Tower in Paris the Brooklyn Bridge in New York City the smoking steelworks of Pittsburgh Pa and the transcontinental railroad with the invention of electric generators and motors and Thomas Edison's light bulb electric power entered home and factory Steel replaced iron for buildings and allowed the erection of skyscrapers The invention of the internal combustion engine led to the arrival of the automobile this in turn fostered the search for petroleum Chemical research provided the impetus for new industries The telephone was invented by Alexander Graham Bell in Farm machinery eased the hard life on the farm and reduced the number of people needed to feed the rest of the population Weapons also changed First the rifled gun barrel was introduced and then the explosive shell that made old fortifications obsolete and finally the machine gun This changed large scale warfare from individual battles to a broad front with millions of soldiers opposing each other by World War I Formal education in prospered with the establishment of engineering colleges throughout the world By the end of the century the world had changed In the developed nations agricultural societies had been replaced by industrial societies machinery the increasing pace of technological change innovating the century makes it difficult to place recent developments into perspective New materials ranging from synthetic rubber through plastics and artificial fabrics have affected ways of life and fashion With the introduction of the electric streetcar in cities extended beyond the distance that could be covered by a horse Following the establishment of the assembly line by Henry Ford in the computer machinery became inexpensive enough for many to afford and changed the landscape in industrialized nations The aircraft industry grew within decades after the first powered flight by the Wright brothers in electronics was ushered in when Marconi sent the first transatlantic radio message in Radio and subsequently television changed communications and entertainment habits Although early computing machines existed by World War it took the invention of the transistor in to make modern computers and office machines a reality Nuclear power was introduced after World War and the space age began with the first Soviet spacecraft in Many of these developments depended on the advances in science that were required before their adaptation by engineers Medical which started with better sanitary practices in the century was expanded by the use of new medicines and new equipment this nearly doubled the life span of a person living in an industrialized country compared to years earlier New technologies in biology led to genetic engineering in which living cells can be altered In weaponry there was the invention of the tank the perfection of the airplane and finally the use of the atomic bomb these changed warfare from what had been primarily an encounter between military personnel to putting all peoples of the world at risk keeps advancing at a rapid rate It can only be guessed what the information revolution of the late century will bring about computerized Assessing Technology It's Effects on Society technology has made modern society possible It has increased the human life span and allowed a healthier life It has added to leisure time and reduced the long hours of work technology can allow the world to feed itself It has reduced the effects of natural catastrophes such as famines and floods The world is now a smaller place where people can readily communicate with each other and travel rapidly anywhere Technology has raised the standard of living at least in the developed nations to a point unimaginable only a century ago Yet a dark side of persists The threat of nuclear war is foremost though other dangers are also frightening The effects of dumping poisonous waste and the continued pollution of the atmosphere are but two examples Although the century has created more jobs than have been lost it still has left many individuals unemployed The world has become smaller but social and political institutions have not kept pace Communication ties together the parts of a society just as the nervous system ties together the parts of an individual From earliest times when the only form of communication was speech to the present when electronic signals carry information instantly to practically any point on Earth communication has been the way people have organized their cooperative activities In the modern world there are two main types of communications media One type consists of the mass planking as television radio newspapers and While which organizations send messages to a large number of people The other type consists of direct point In telegraph data transmission and postal service Of these the electronic media all but the postal service are termed telecommunications Telecommunication first came into existence with the development of the telegraph in the s and s For the first time news and information could be transmitted great distances almost instantaneously The invention of the telephone in by Alexander Graham Bell fundamentally transformed telecommunications The telephone system assumed its modern form with the development of dial phoning and its spread during the middle decades of the th century Telegraph Telephone After however a new transformation of telecommunications began The used to carry information changed radically At the same time ordinary telephone and telegraph traffic was enormously supplemented by huge masses of computer data as millions of computers were tied together into global networks in most cases telecommunications systems transmit information by wire radio or space satellite. computerized. Wire transmission involves sending electrical signals over various types of wire lines such as open wire self contained cable and coaxial cable These lines can be used to transmit voice frequencies telegraph messages Floppy disk data and television programs Another somewhat related transmission medium that has come into increasingly wider use especially in telephone communications is a type of cable composed of optical fibers Here electrical signals converted to light signals by a noon transmitter carry both speech and data over bundles of thin glass or plastic filaments Radio communications systems transmit electronic signals in relatively narrow frequency bands through the air They include radio navigation and both amateur and commercial broadcasting Commercial broadcasting consists of AM FM and TV broadcasting for general public use Satellite communications allow the exchange of television or telephone signals between widely separated locations by means of microwaves that is very short radio waves with wavelengths from inches to inch centimeters to centimeter, which correspond to a frequency range of to gigahertz GHz or to billion cycles per second Since satellite systems do not require the construction of intermediate relay or repeater stations as do ground based microwave systems they can be put into service much more rapidly Modern telecommunications networks thus not only send the traditional voice communications of telephones and the printed messages of telegraphs and telexes they also carry images the still images of facsimile machines or the moving images of video television transmissions used in videoconferences in which the participants can see as well as hear each other Additionally they carry encoded data ranging from the business accounts of a multinational corporation to medical data relayed for analysis by physicians thousands of miles from a patient added services during the late s and s a number of new telecommunications services came into existence that transmitted information in forms other than voice or printed material Videoconferencing for example became increasingly popular with businesses In a videoconference participants gather in specially equipped rooms in different places often in different cities The rooms have microphones and a number of television cameras and screens Voice signals and images from the room in which a person is speaking are transmitted over high capacity links to all the other rooms in the other places Thus all participants can both hear and see the speaker and in most such systems see projected on a screen whatever charts or diagrams the speaker is using In videoconferencing as in all the related services signals are converted to digital form before being transmitted In addition coding patterns are used to compress the amount of data sent For example instead of sending a signal for each part of a given image a signal is sent only when an image changes in some way   Another new service was videotexts Here a user can send requests for specific types of information over a telephone generally by pushing buttons and the information transmitted over telephone or cable television lines can be displayed on a television receiver equipped with a special decoder   most important service one that expanded rapidly from the s was data transmission which links computers directly with other computers locally or worldwide through a telecommunications network This can be done in many different ways The simplest method is to attach individual computers to the telephone network through devices called modems translate data from a computer into a code that is carried by the telephone link to other computers with their own modems The Internet an international network of millions of computers offers bulletin boards electronic mail systems file transfer and other online services in more sophisticated computer networks dedicated computers that is computers programmed to carry out only one or a limited number of functionary used for switching messages They allow messages from one computer to be broadcast to all others simultaneously Such systems also allow for data to be stored within the network for forwarding at a later time Multinational corporations especially major banks credit corporations and airlines depend upon such systems In all cases the means of data transmission are the same as those used in the rest of the telecommunications systems

Microwave links satellite communications and fiber optics carry such data transfers   Data however generally require higher rates of transmission Special connections must frequently be made to the various computers to allow for sufficient carrying capacity This means that changes in a data transmission system often require costly rewiring and entirely new redesigned equipment in contrast to the telephone system in which new phone units can be added relatively inexpensively Computer Satellite Telecommunications Industry Until the s the world telecommunications system had a relatively simple administrative structure In the   telephone service was supplied by a regulated monopoly   Telephone and Telegraph AT&T Telegraph service was provided mainly by the Western Union Corporation In almost all other countries both services were the monopolies of government agencies known for post telephone and telegraph   In the however beginning in the situation became far more complex As a result of an antitrust suit launched by the federal government AT&T agreed in a court settlement to divest itself of the local operating companies that provided basic telephone service They remained regulated local monopolies grouped together into eight regional companies AT&T now offers long distance service in competition with a half dozen major and many minor competitors while retaining ownership of a subsidiary that produces telephone equipment computers and other electronic devices during the same period Great Britain's national telephone company was sold to private investors as was Peters telephone monopoly forming telegraphy and data transmission Western Union was joined by many other major companies while many leading multinational firms formed their own telecommunications services that link offices scattered throughout the world   New also brought continuing changes in the providers of telecommunications private companies such as Comsat in the were organized to provide satellite communications links within the country An international organization called Intelsat which is jointly owned by the various PTTs and private communications companies furnished the global links in the satellite telecommunications network the introduction of more widespread competition into the highly integrated telecommunications networks proved a controversial move Supporters praised it as a way of liberating the field from monopolistic practices that retarded and kept rates uneconomically high But critics pointed out at least in the early years of deregulation that rates for the vast majority of users rose sharply and that in so respects technical progress became electronics. Television stereophonic recording and playback the computer robots and space probes are all products of a single basic : electronics is the use of electricity to control communicate and process information Its products have caused greater changes in everyday life than those of any other in the second half of the th century   The electronic signal   The basis of electronics is the electronic signal an electric current that represents information There are two basic types of electrical signals: analog and digital In analog signals some continuously variable aspect of the electrical current represents the information   In amplitude modulated AM radio transmissions for example the amplitude or strength of the electromagnetic radio wave is proportional to the amplitude of the signal the volume of the sound that the radio wave carries The greater the amplitude of the radio wave the louder the sound that radiates from the radio speaker surging contrast digital signals use standardized pulses to represent numbers With a digital audio signal the amplitude of the signal for a set amount of time is converted to a number represented by for example pulses of fixed duration and amplitude The audio signal as a whole is transmitted as a series of such pulse codes   Most electronic devices deal with digital signals In these signals the numbers are almost always represented in a binary code that is instead of using a number system based on as is used in writing numbers and manual arithmetic electronic systems use numbers based on There are only two basic numbers in this system: and with being represented by a pulse and by the absence of a pulse or some similar arrangement the number in the base system for example would be represented in the base two system by meaning numerical grounding alphabetical and words can be encoded in much the same manner as can be logic codes such as zero meaning no and meaning yes semi conducting Devices electronic devices that manipulate digital and analog signals are predominantly semiconductors in today's semiconductor is a material that conducts electricity but only under certain conditions in contrast with conductors that always conduct well and insulators that always conduct poorly Semiconductors are generally made of silicon or silicon compounds that are doped with certain impurities to alter their electrical properties the basic semiconductor device is the transistor invented in by scientists William B Shockley Walter H Brattain and John Bardeen The typical transistor consists of three semiconductor materials bonded together In the so called upon type the first part called the emitter is doped to give it an excess of negative charges the second the base is doped to give it excess positive charges and the third the collector is doped to give it an excess of negative charges Peter   The voltage applied between the emitter and collector is fixed and relatively high while the voltage between the emitter and the base is low and variable integrative is the incoming signal When there is no base voltage the resistance from the emitter to the collector is high and no current flows small voltage across the base to the emitter however lowers the resistance and allows a large output current to flow from emitter to collector The transistor thus acts as a signal amplifier   transistor electronic circuits   transistors and other semiconductor devices come in a wide variety of types capable of performing many different functions when linked together with other elements into electronic circuits The most important of these other elements are resistors which impede the flow of electrons and regulate voltages and currents conductors which connect different circuits or different circuit elements together and capacitors which store electrical charges the functions that such circuits perform are generally of two broad types logic circuits transform or process information carried by electronic signals, while memory circuits and devices store the information Logic circuits are built up out of identical components that perform elementary manipulations on each piece of information called a bit consists of either a or a Sometimes another unit of information known as a byte or eight bits is also used There are three basic types of logic circuits inserting circuits are combined with magnetism circuits to make negotiating adaptable circuits innovating gate two inputs produce an output only if both inputs are In other words the output says Both and B are true or Similarly the OR gate produces an output if either of its two inputs paralyze technology navigation distorting gates do just the opposite produces an output allowing accessible compression in any case where the gate produces equally concealment produces whenever OR produces Put together these simple circuits can perform any logical or arithmetic operation that can be defined in a finite number of steps the fastest memory circuits are built up from arrays of transistors as are logic circuits In memory circuits a transient impulse the information to be stored is directed to a particular unit or address in the array This impulse changes the electrical state of a simple circuit in such a way that the change is stable once the impulse has passed one simple way of making such a flip flop circuit is to have the output of a given transistor feed back to its base through an OR gate The other input to the OR gate is the external pulse single external pulse will turn on the transistor output current which will feed back through the gate to maintain itself An additional external pulse will turn the input off thus flipping the circuit back Information can be obtained from complex arrays of flip flop circuits by various means in which the transistor signals to external circuits whether it is in a conducting or a non conducting state Such arrays are termed random access memories or rams because each of the addresses can be accessed in any order other types of memory circuits include read only memories or ROMs here the data is permanently stored in the array at the time of its manufacture semiconductors may someday be replaced in logic circuits at least for some applications requiring extreme speed Researchers are developing new electronic devices based on superconductive materials When certain materials are cooled to near absolute zero, their resistance to the flow of electrons disappears entirely allowing them to become superconductors These new devices called Josephson junctions are many times faster and smaller than the smallest possible semiconductor In the late s the discovery of a new class of high temperature superconductors led to the belief that a low cost alternative to expensive cooling techniques was within reach storage devices not all electronic devices are based on semiconductors Many important types of information storage media are based instead on magnetic materials In computers the most widely used form of storage is the magnetic disk in which the bits of information are stored in strips of magnetic materials laid in concentric circles around the disk Each bit of information to be stored is coded as a left right or right left magnetic field and impressed onto the disk by a recording head which is a form of electromagnet the rapidly spinning disk is read by the head which moves quickly to the appropriate part of the disk and detects the magnetic fields in a given region Magnetic tape is also used for storing computer and broadcast information as well such as in video and audio recording tape recorder the most recently developed type of information storage is the magneto optical disk The disk is made of a special magnetic material that can easily change its magnetic orientation only when heated by a small laser The laser is focused at the point at which information is recorded and a magnetic field is impressed

Another laser can read the field by bouncing light off the disk The polarization of the light the direction in which the electrical and magnetic fields making up the light vibrate is changed by the magnetic field and such changes can be detected by polarized filters and photo detectors This optical and magnetic allows many billions of bytes to be stored on a single disk electronic tubes for producing radio and radar signals electronic tubes are often used though tube is no longer applied to switching circuits as it was in the early days of electronics Two common types are magnetrons and klystrons Both are partially evacuated sealed tubes magnetron tube has a cylindrical anode and a single wire filament running along the cylinder axis which emits the electrons The tube is mounted inside a magnet whose field runs parallel to the filament Electrons starting from the filament are bent into curved paths by the magnetic field and their oscillations emit radio radiation Magnetrons are capable of generating extremely high frequencies and also short bursts of very high power they are an important source of power in radar systems and in microwave ovens klystron tube contains hollow copper cavities within which the electrons oscillate Klystrons are used in ultrahigh frequency circuits where they can produce oscillations up to megahertz megacycles per second in the short microwave range Another important type of electronic vacuum device is the cathode ray tube which is used in television receivers among many other applications the cathode ray tube is a two electrode tube in which the electrons are focused by a system of electric lenses into a fine beam This beam falls on a fluorescent screen at the end of the tube where it produces a spot of light If an electric field is applied at right angles to the direction of the beam the paths of the electrons which first followed a straight line are bent. This displacement is a measure of the strength of the applied field The cathode ray tube can be used as a voltmeter a device that measures electric potential difference If the field applied to the deflecting plates is an alternating field the light point moves constantly over the screen from right to left and back This appears as a straight horizontal line If another alternating field operates at right angles to the first one and to the electron beam the light point is at the same time pulled up and down and a more complicated figure is seen on the screen This permits study in detail of the relation of frequencies phases and amplitudes of the two fields   If however one of the fields operates so that the light point is slowly moved over the screen from left to right and returned very fast to the left the viewer gets a simple picture of the properties of the second field which moves the spot up and down cathode ray tube of this type is called an oscilloscope integrated circuits Despite the importance of these other types of electronic devices semiconductor based circuits are the essential feature of modern electronic equipment These circuits are not made up of individual separated components as was once the case Instead thousands of tiny circuits are embedded in a single complex piece of silicon and other materials called an integrated circuit IC   Peter manufactured of integrated circuits begins with a simple circular wafer of silicon a few inches across Designers have produced drawings of exactly where each element in the finished circuits is to go Usually these diagrams are themselves made with the help of computers Photographs of the diagrams are then reduced in size many times to produce a photolithographic mask The wafers are first coated with a material called a photo resist that undergoes a chemical change when exposed to light shone through the mask onto the photo resist creates the same pattern on the wafer as that on the mask Solvents then etch away the parts of the resist exposed to light leaving the other parts intact after this another layer of material for example silicon doped with some impurities is laid down on top of the wafer and another pattern is etched in by the same technique The result of several such operations is a multilayered circuit with thousands of tiny transistors resistors and conductors created in the wafer   The wafer is then broken apart along prostheses lines into dozens of identical square or rectangular chips the finished integrated circuits During the s and s advancing reduced the size of individual circuit elements by a factor of two every two years leading in the same period to a fourfold increase in the number of elements that can fit on a chip This rapid increase in the power of the chips and the simultaneous rise in their speed allowed the development of microprocessors which are at the heart of millions of personal and home computers pack the same computing power into a tiny chip a fraction of an inch on a side that years earlier would have been provided by a computer that filled a whole room and cost many millions of dollars individual chips are mounted on carriers with several dozen connector leads emerging from them These in turn are soldered together onto printed circuit boards that may contain many dozens of chips In large computers the boards themselves are mounted into large racks and again connected together computerized. By the minds integrated circuits made with the most advanced could carry as many as a million individual transistors each only a few microns on a side micron is a thousandth of a millimeter or inch Many electrical engineers and scientists believe that the ultimate limits of size in these circuits might soon be reached. Computerized combining was expected that the circuit elements would become too small and contain too few individual atoms to be manufactured reliably Peter continue the reduction in size and cost of microcircuits new principles of operation may be required perhaps involving specially designed organic molecules applications integrated circuits are extremely versatile because a single basic design can be made to perform hundreds of different functions depending on the wiring of the circuits and the electronic programs or instructions that are fed into them *see* Computer Most ICs perform calculations or logic manipulations in devices ranging from handheld calculators to ultra fast supercomputers that can perform billions of calculations per second There are many other functions however that can be done with electronic circuitry In radio and television receivers a primary function of circuits is the amplification of weak signals received by the antenna In amplification a small signal is magnified to a large signal that is used to drive other circuits such as the speakers of a radio converting many cases this amplification is performed with the help of oscillator circuits Such circuits have a natural period or cycle of electrical current similar to the natural beat of a pendulum When driven by external signals of the same period such as the transmission from a particular radio channel the oscillator circuit increases its amplitude of oscillation To tune out other radio or television stations also received by a single antenna filter circuits are frequently used Such filters strongly reduce the signals at all but a single frequency preventing interference among channels in a receiver these and other basic circuit types are used in a vast array of electronic devices Consumer electronics a field that was first developed in the century with the invention of the phonograph now includes radios television sets high fidelity stereo systems tape recorders calculators video games and personal computers Most of these devices contain one or more integrated circuits Electronic controls have also been added to many electrical appliances such as dishwashers washing machines ovens and food processors. In industry and trade the computer made up of from one to several thousand integrated circuits has become an invaluable tool controlling industrial operations and keeping track of voluminous business records When connected to mechanical arms and grippers electronics is the brain of the industrial robot that has come into increasingly widespread use for painting welding and assembling products that range from automobiles to watches scientists use electronic computers to perform extremely complex calculations such as determining exactly the course of distant space probes the probes themselves are packed with electronic instruments and communications equipment Electronic instruments are used on Earth for scientific measurements and in the electronics industry itself to test equipment as it is manufactured The oscilloscope for example is used to diagnose problems in electronic circuits through a comparison of expected test patterns with actual results. Computerized Innovative fields of terminology electronic diagnostic instruments have given physicians a much clearer view of the human body than ever before Computerized axial tomography CAT scanners which are a sophisticated form of X-ray machines use computers to analyze X rays and produce three dimensional views of internal organs Nuclear magnetic resonance scanners analyze the response of the body's chemicals to radio waves and magnetic fields producing maps of the body's biochemistry and clearly highlighting areas of disease Virtually all modern communications rely on electronics Electronic circuits switch telephone calls both on Earth and in communications satellites Satellite electronics systems amplify and retransmit television and radio communications Computers are tied together by electronic networks   Conventional electronics is now supplemented in communications by optoelectronics the use of laser light carried by optical fibers to transmit information at high speed Laser pulses are modulated by electronic signals and the light at the other end of the fiber many kilometers away is converted back into electronic signals by photo detectors   Electronics has also come to play a central role in transportation ICs are used in the engines of almost all new cars acting to control the engine and to use fuel efficiently Much more complex circuits and computers greatly assist pilots in flying transport aircraft and are of course even more vital when used in space such as on board space shuttles   Finally electronics has come to be central in modern warfare and preparations for war Nearly half the cost of advanced fighter aircraft is in the sophisticated electronic radar weapons control and automated missiles carried by the planes Electronic computers and navigation equipment guide ballistic nuclear missiles on their paths and control the detonation of nuclear weapons computerized The working principles of electronics can be demonstrated by tracing the history of radio tubes and photoelectric cells The history began in when Thomas Edison found that the heated filament in his incandescent lamp gave off material that blackened the inside of the bulb This was called the Edison effect and it led to the development of the modern radio tube In the Edison effect also called thermion emission heat supplies some electrons in the filament with at least the minimal energy to overcome the attractive forces holding them in the structure of the metal This discharge of electrons is widely used as a source of electrons in conventional electron tubes for example in television picture tubes Peter exampled proven existence of radio waves discovered the photoelectric effect If polished metal is given a negative charge and then is flooded with ultraviolet radiation it steadily loses the charge Some chemical elements such as cesium and selenium are sensitive to visible light This discovery led to photoelectric cells The development of the radio tube began in when John Fleming of England produced the Fleming valve which today is called a diode meaning two electrodes Peter started by heating a filament also called a cathode in a vacuum tube with circuit current The heat drove electrons out of the filament and into surrounding space nothing more happened the first electrons to escape would soon have formed a negative space charge that would have kept others from being driven out because like charges repel Fleming avoided this by placing a plate in the tube and connecting the plate and filament through an outside B circuit The electrons driven from the filament then crossed the tube to the plate and followed the circuit back to the filament Peter next placed a battery in the B circuit The battery was used to supply electrons that is negative charges to the filament or cathode and draw them from the plate or anode leaving a positive charge Electrical heating drove electrons steadily from the filament and sent a strong current through the B or plate circuit The strength of the current depends partly upon the heat and partly upon the voltage from the battery This device could be used as a radio detector The changing voltages created by radio signals in an antenna circuit are placed on the filament and plate The changes produce corresponding changes in the strength of the plate current which is used to reproduce the signal in the receiving apparatus inventions transformed the diode into a device that he called an audio the modern name of which is triode He did this by inserting a grid of fine wire mesh between the filament and the plate If variable voltages from an antenna circuit are placed on the filament and the grid they cause variations in the flow of electrons to the plate Moreover the variations in current are much stronger than those caused by the voltage of the incoming signal acting alone Thus the triode amplifies or strengthens the signal because the tube uses free electrons only and has no mechanical moving parts it responds within a few microseconds or millionths of a second to any change placed upon it can be made sensitive to changes of less than a millionth of a volt Resulting changes in the plate current can be amplified by passing the signal through more tubes The vacuum tube became the basis of radio television and computers the latter first developed at the end of World War II in and The invention of the transistor in initiated a radical reduction in the size of electronic circuits and in their power requirements The later development of the integrated circuit set into motion the continuing miniaturization of all electronic devices which has at the same time greatly increased their speed and computing power humans incessantly explore experiment create and examine the world The active process by which physical biological and social phenomena are studied is known as science Individuals involved in science called scientists often spend their entire lives in pursuit of answers to probing questions This ongoing process often leads to new areas of scientific inquiry Although many areas of scientific inquiry are interrelated specific scientific disciplines or divisions have been established The three broad divisions of science are the physical sciences biological or life sciences and social science. Some scientists are driven by little more than the desire to learn They may study to gain knowledge for its own sake These scientists are engaged in basic or pure science Their projects may or may not have any relevance to everyday life Scientists working in applied science on the other hand usually have a specific goal in mind This goal may involve a product process business or other human need An applied scientist often uses information recently gathered by other scientists as well as the cumulative knowledge of the pure sciences The significance of science in society plays a major role erupting Peters discoveries however even nonscientists can appreciate scientific progress Because of science human understanding of the past present and future is constantly in a state of flux For instance decades ago the notion of landing a spacecraft on the moon would have seemed an impossible feat today it is a mark of scientific progress Because scientific inquiry never ceases to exist events once dismissed as material for science fiction such as landing on Mars now seem inevitable Science can be found in nearly all aspects of everyday life for instance if electricity had never been discovered electric appliances heaters lights and television would not exist Electronic components found in radios televisions watches and calculators are now smaller and more reliable than before Advances in electronics are responsible for what is called the computer age Because of computer information can be processed in seconds At one time computers were extremely expensive They were rarely found outside of laboratories and large businesses since they are now more economically made computers can be found in many homes schools stores and libraries Computers facilitate travel plans by providing travel agents with easy access to flight schedules prices and seating availability Businesses use computers to track inventory purchase and sell stocks calculate payrolls and perform many other functions Computers are also used as educational devices in schools to monitor home heating systems and to guide satellites and space probes In the future computers may have microprocessors produced in outer space because the environment there is devoid of the Earth's dust and gravitational force computer electronics microprocessor Radio Television In physics the discovery of nuclear energy has had a tremendous effect on the world. computerized It is used in nuclear weapons and in some areas provides electricity for homes In the past few decades physicists also have revised their notion of the atom They once thought of the atom as the elementary building block of matter Using particle accelerators it was determined that atoms themselves are composed of many types of elementary particles held together by special forces Atomic particles nuclear energy Physicists also have invented sophisticated lasers that produce concentrated beams of light Lasers are used in medicine industry communications navigation and in the military *see* Laser and Maser In the late s scientists working in the area of physical chemistry produced a new class of superconducting materials in the laboratory Theoretically an electric current can run forever through a superconductor provided that the superconducting temperature is maintained These so called high temperature superconductors have many potential applications in particle accelerators computers power transmission lines and magnetically levitated super fast trains cryogenics super fluidity and superconductivity the battle against disease and illness has also gained much from science Safer surgical procedures are now in use including those for organ transplantation and coronary bypass surgery Many procedures have been improved because of the development of specialized medical instruments Some instruments enable physicians to see inside the body without making a single incision Others can carry out essential bodily functions such as pumping blood or breathing Medical researchers are making progress toward the production of artificial blood which may eventually eliminate the threat of contracting diseases transmitted during blood transfusions One such disease is acquired immune deficiency syndrome also known as fatal disease attacks the human immune system rendering it incapable of warding off infections Many other scientific advances have provided humans with the ability to significantly alter the environment scientists now know that the release of certain synthetic chemical compounds into the air can cause hazardous atmospheric changes such as the destruction of the ozone layer It is feared that damage to the ozone layer would allow increased amounts of ultraviolet radiation from the sun to penetrate the atmosphere and cause a large increase in the rate compression materials It is also known that the burning of fossil fuels adds a great deal of carbon dioxide to the atmosphere which has the effect of trapping the sun's heat the greenhouse effect With a constant increase in the average temperature of the atmosphere ice sheets at the North and South poles would melt increasing the amount of water in the oceans It is feared that this would lead to a higher sea level and cause flooding in perfected legible areas servicing order to gain further information about these potentially dangerous situations scientists monitor the ozone layer and atmospheric carbon dioxide and study computer generated images gathered by satellite Another mark of scientific advancement is the improved understanding of the world's limited supply of petroleum Concern about the world's future energy needs have resulted in the study of alternative energy resources which include solar energy nuclear energy wind energy wave energy and energy from the earth's own internal heat energy solving Problems Scientifically minded people generally believe in cause and effect relationships they feel there is a perfectly natural explanation for most things For example there is a reason why milk sours and why some leaves turn red in the fall while others turn yellow Changes such as these which are easily observed are known as phenomena Some common phenomena are not completely understood still others cannot be explained at all at this time The belief that effects have causes plays a significant part in the scientific method The cause of inserting higher Methodism for example was once unknown Nevertheless scientists firmly believed that a cause existed Once they discovered that it was caused by a virus scientists could search for a remedy If everyone believed that a disease just happened without a natural cause no progress would be made in learning to control it Disease Human Vaccines Virus Scientists spend tremendous amounts of time making observations and gathering information or data They work using the scientific method Scientists may first become intrigued with a specific problem They learn about these problems in a variety of ways Sometimes they discover them through chance observation Awareness may also result from reading from laboratory experiments or simply from thinking Once the problem is firmly grasped the scientist tries to learn as much as possible about it Frequently this involves studying books and journals that contain information about the problem This is called searching the literature After data has been collected and analyzed the scientist formulates an educated guess called a hypothesis The scientist then designs experiments to test the hypothesis The experiment may involve designing a theoretical model to be simulated and tested by a computer Whatever form the experiment takes the scientist must obtain measurements or other data from the experiment Analysis of the data will either suggest the validity of the hypothesis or suggest a revision of the hypothesis Once revised and retested the hypothesis may gain the acceptance of other scientists with similar interests They will repeat the experiment to retest the validity of the hypothesis An idea model or explanation that has been rigorously tested analyzed and accepted by the scientific community is called a theory The theory will continue to be an accepted explanation unless new information is uncovered that the scientific community agrees disproves it The continuous scrutiny under which scientists operate helps to avoid errors Science Humans have always been curious about their surroundings One of the most fundamental quests is the explanation of human origin and destiny Perhaps this is where natural philosophy beginning the search for the relationship between humans and the universe All societies have tried to explain the origin of humans and their role in nature These questions have been addressed by philosophers religious scholars and scientists alike   Religion has had a tremendous influence on the discoveries and opinions of the scientific communist naturalized philosophy Peter for example had tremendous difficulty convincing the Roman Catholic church of the truth of his astronomical findings His idea of a sun centered heliocentric solar system contradicted the Earth centered geocentric model accepted by the church He was put on trial for sharing his observations and he spent parts of his life under close supervision because of his ideas Another historic controversy centers on the age of the Earth Many religious traditions set the Earth's age at about years However scientists believe the Earth is much older billion years old In both examples science and religion have differed in the way they gather information about the world Like philosophy science emphasizes the use of logic In fact science can be viewed as a scrutinizing system of logic It seeks to answer questions by observing phenomena The scientific method is the system of logic used by scientists though some sciences differ in their use of logic As scientists try to solve a problem they may use a model based on a logical plausible connection of events Like a hypothesis the model is then tested by making predictions based on the model If the predictions are proven wrong then the model is revised If the model survives the tests the model becomes the system of logic that describes the theory Theoretical models of this nature have been used to study economics the structure of the atom the universe evolution and even the origin of life   Unlike philosophy science emphasizes the repeatability of results This means that a given set of circumstances should always produce the same result scientific theories are not accepted by the scientific community until the theory has been validated One way to validate a theory is to have scientists in other laboratories duplicate the experiment or the calculations Using another set of materials and methods these scientists may repeat the experiment and check the accuracy of the previous report This long and careful process will confirm that the original result was not merely a fluke occurrence a misinterpretation of events or an error in procedure By having several scientists investigate a situation the most accurate description of cause and effect can be determined Many of the most basic questions in science can be phrased in the formidable actionist stating questions What determines These allocation attempting towards establishing causable affections   difficulty arises when many factors or variables affect the system at one time variable is something that has different values under different conditions In one type of laboratory test all the variables but one are controlled The uncontrolled variable is known as the experimental variable and the others are the control variables This method of testing is called controlled experimentation science was unknown for thousands of years before the dawn of recorded history Nevertheless many significant discoveries and inventions were made during this prescience time One of these discoveries was that fire could be harnessed and put to work Fire While some extensions have an instinctive fear of fire possessions somehow discovered that fire could be controlled and kept in one place tabulating chemical reactions formulating answers involving product delusions exactly when this discovery was first made however archaeologists have found that during the humans used fire for cooking and to keep warm Today this very same source of heat is used to produce steam for turbines early hunting methods and agriculture Early humans also used fire to help hunt and kill animals for food One method used called the fire drive enabled a few people to kill several animals without a great deal of work First animals had to be found grazing near a cliff during the summer when grass was dry Then when the wind was blowing in the right direction a few hunters set fire to the dry grass with torches The flames drove the animals over the cliff By using fire in this way early hunters had more to eat after a small amount of work than they would have had after a full week of hunting with a spear or club For a long time humans roamed across the land hunting wild animals for food Eventually doglike creatures were noticed to have an instinctive ability to detect game even when the hunters could not see it These creatures often followed the hunters and they were gradually trained to find game for the hunters to kill Then dog and hunter would share the spoils of the hunt In time humans realized that other wild animals could also be domesticated and kept for human use They also found that they did not have to travel great distances to gather edible plants could be grown where they were needed Soon humans began to raise crops   other early discoveries Primitive methods of tanning leather and spinning and weaving were probably discovered at about this time   Leather Spinning and Weaving Humans also learned how to make clay pots in which to store things Perhaps the accidental exposure of such a pot to a fire resulted in the first pottery These clay pots could not be used for cooking however because clay whether burned or not is a poor conductor of heat Instead round stones were put in an open fire When they were red hot they were scooped up with a wooden or clay ladle and dumped into a pot of water The stones would then heat the water and cook the food This primitive method of cooking was still used in some areas until the beginning of the th century Another early invention was the wheel The inspiration for the wheel may have come from using logs as rollers to move heavy objects Whatever the origin the wheel was readily adapted to a variety of uses Placed horizontally a wheel was an aid in making pottery though its greatest value was its use on primitive carts for carrying heavy loads Waterwheels were devised as tools for lifting water and windmills became power sources Wheel One of the first metals put to use by early human beings was copper Like gold and silver this metal is sometimes found in pure form Since it is so malleable it can also be hammered into various shapes without first being heated Man probably discovered how to heat ore and smelt metals by accident mixture of tin and copper produced the first bronze This was widely used Copper Bronze Tin Having learned that ores could be smelted man probably tried the process on many different substances Often the work was wasted but occasionally the result was useful Glass was possibly discovered in this way Soon after the smelting of metals became common metal money was probably invented Pieces of money with a fixed value made trade and commerce possible Copper was used for the least valuable pieces silver for the more valuable coins and gold for the most valuable Money The Beginning of Writing began in Mesopotamia and Egypt several thousand years before the time of Christ Egypt Ancient Mesopotamia Picture writing was probably the first method of setting down what man saw heard or felt This was called pictographic writing It was many centuries before any kind of alphabet was developed Alphabet Writing By the time writing began all the abovementioned discoveries and many more had been made Their use however was not scientific The tanner for example did not really know what happened to a piece of skin which he converted into useful leather His knowledge of the tanner's art had simply been learned from his father and grandfather He knew what to do but not why he did it Glassmakers and men who smelted metals had no knowledge of the chemistry involved in the processes they used This was true of artisans of all kinds They were highly skilled craftsmen but they had no idea of the scientific principles involved in their art or trade   Writing made possible the beginning of science It enabled man to record what one generation of people

science Their road building feats were not equaled until modern times They made the first road maps with distances between stations along their roads carefully measured in paces They built great aqueducts to carry water over long distances   Roads and Streets Roman Empire The period from the end of the Roman Empire to about AD is often called the Dark Ages There was not much progress made in Europe during this period The foundations were laid however for important advances that were to follow in the later Middle Ages and the Renaissance The stirrup was probably invented during the Dark Ages Water wheels also made their first appearance then They were used as sources of power in small rivers and in sea inlets where they were run by tidal currents The water wheel led to the windmill which was introduced in about The magnetic compass was also invented at about this time   Compass Magnetic Papermaking assembly distributed sorting material inserting chemical distant accumulations compressing materials in chemical segments. By the century papermaking spread throughout Europe Paper was a Chinese invention It had been adopted by the Persians and then by the Arabs who brought the art to Europe Paper   Powder not gunpowder because guns were not yet known and fireworks rockets were introduced into Europe in the s They had been invented in Peters laboratorial some years earliest the earliest mention of firearms is in a Dutch chronicle dated It states that firearms were invented in America The first picture of a primitive cannon can be found in an English manuscript dated   Rocket Explosive Firearms   Gutenberg's Contribution In the century Peter developed a practical method of printing Peter had converted movable type in the century but made little use of it printing computerized printing method started a new era in the growth of science Before Peter a student might spend a whole year copying a book by hand After Peter recreations were printed much more quickly They were also available in large enough quantities for universities to expand their libraries for the increased use of both faculty and students It was due mainly to the existence of the printed book that the great scientists of the century could work systematically Books made both old and new knowledge readily available Anybody who truly wanted to learn could now do so because books could be easily circulated from person to person In spite of the rather large number of books that were written and printed in the century most of the sciences remained in their earliest stage This earliest stage is the collection of everything that is known in a certain field then reviewing that material or commenting on it does not include an explanation of why things are the way they are sciences exhumes exampled pioneer work in anatomy He named every bone muscle and most of the blood vessels in the body He did not know however how the human body functioned listed all the known to man but he had no idea of the relationships of the various animals to one another Agricola Georg Bauer wrote about the mining of metals and the processing of ores but he knew nothing about chemistry Gunnery masteries written conductivity a book on guns and shooting but he knew nothing of ballistics placing a historic book on astronomy was published It was 'Concerning the Revolutions sphere binding formative centuries the science of astronomy had been based on the Ptolemaic theory that the Earth was the center of the universe and motionless The problem was to explain how the other planets and heavenly bodies moved At first it was thought that they simply moved in circular orbits around the Earth calculations based on this view however did not agree with actual observations Then it was thought that the other planets traveled in small circular orbits These in turn were believed to move along larger orbits around the Earth With this theory however it could not be proved that the Earth was the center of the universe entries his historic book copernicus said that the Earth should be regarded as one of the planets which revolved around the sun Peter also stated that the Earth rotated on an axis copernicus however still clung to the ideas of planets traveling in small circular orbits which moved along larger orbits although it was revolutionary Copernicus' theory did not offer an adequate explanation of the movement of the planets This explanation came more than a half century later Peters laws of planetary motion list years trying to work out the probative of the planet Mars by means of a small circle epicycle moving along a larger one around the sun No matter how he tried it did not work After six years of study he came to realize that the movement of Mars could be understood To do this one had to assume that the planet moved along an elliptical oval orbit at a speed which varied according to the planet's distance from the sun now all the observations fitted Peters stabilities concerning functional surface laser portions then could write down the following first two laws on which all modern astronomy is based the path of every planet in motion around the sun forms an ellipse with the sun at one focus The speed of a planet in its orbit varies so that a line joining it with the sun sweeps over equal areas in equal times The second law means that a planet moves faster when close to the sun and more slowly when it is farther away Later Peter also set down a third law of planetary motion It deals with the relationship between the distance of a planet from the sun and the time a planet takes to complete one orbit while Peter was working out his laws of planetary motion Galileo Galilee proved that Copernicus was right in stating that the Earth moved on its axis Galileo He did this using a telescope Peter affiliate marketing eyeglasses had assorted a cubical which made distant things look near although Peter knew very little about this primitive telescope he made one himself Using it he discovered that the planet Jupiter had moons satellites He also saw that the planet Venus passed through phases as does the Earth's moon This indicated that Venus moved around the sun inside the Earth's orbit He saw too that the Milky Way was made up of countless distant stars Galileo's observations led him to conclude that copernicus had been right in at least part of his theories regarding astronomy telescope Peters discoveries had been able to show how a planet moves later in the century showed why it travels the way it does wondered where the power to move a planet came from having found that the motion of the planet was faster near the sun he had speculated that the driving power might come from the sun   Newton showed that there were always two forces at work These were the inertia of a body and the attraction between bodies Peters great discovery 'Principia' appeared in Modern scientific have observed that in this book Newton developed the theory of artificial Earth satellites He also developed the theory that a rocket should operate in a vacuum electricity While Copernicus Peter Galileo and Newton were establishing astronomy as a science material for other sciences was still just being accumulated For example Otto von Guericke of Magdeburg Germany invented a primitive way of making electricity He took an ordinary grindstone and substituted a ball of sulfur for the stone With one hand he cranked the ball With the other he rubbed it The friction created static electricity Wax and amber balls were also used Newton improved upon this method by substituting a glass ball for one of sulfur In Stephen Gray in England discovered that electricity could be conducted through metal rods At this point man's knowledge of electricity stopped growing because of some mistaken ideas about it The substances which could be used to produce electricity sulfur glass wax and amber were called electrics They could be used to produce electricity but they would not conduct it The metal conductors which Gray had discovered would conduct electricity but they could not produce it was now reasoned that a substance had to be an electric or a conductor The proper distinction of course would have been insulators and conductors and a conductor could be used to produce electricity if it was insulated Electricity Mathematics Two very important mathematical developments took place during the century In logarithms It had been possible to do long multiplication and division problems before the invention of logarithms With logarithms up to per cent of the time required for a given calculation could be saved Near the end of the century Newton in England and Gottfried Wilhelm von Leibnitz in Germany were key figures in the development of calculus Logarithms were mostly timesavers Calculus permitted the solution of certain types of problems These calculations would have been completely impossible without its aid calculus he century saw the development of a practical device as important and far reaching in its results as had been the invention of movable type This was the steam engine a device as interesting for physics as it was useful for industry Steam Engine In order to understand the importance of the steam engine it is necessary to understand an engineering term The term is firm power which means simply power when and where it is wanted large windmill can be quite powerful but it provides force only if a wind happens to be blowing water wheel comes closer to supplying firm power but there is little choice in its location the steam engine provided firm power It could be built anywhere The only problem might be the transportation of fuel to make it run The earliest known form of steam engine was the machine built by Hero of Alexandria in the century This device was called an oeuvre and it worked on the same principle as a lawn sprinkler using steam rather than water Jet Propulsion In imaginary the steam turbine It worked by blowing a jet of steam against a kind of modified structural symbolic wheel Neither of these machines was powerful enough to do any useful work The first useful steam engine was invented components were known as a pumping engine because it had been invented for the specific purpose of pumping insulation projector mine shafts In this engine the hose which was to suck up the distance led into a large container that had just been filled with steam Then the steam valve was closed and a stream of cold water was run onto the metal container The steam inside condensed

This produced a partial vacuum and water was sucked into the container The water was then drained from it In production an atmospheric engine which had a piston connected to a large crossbeam Steam was put into the cylinder to raise the piston Next cold water was sprayed into the cylinder condensing the steam The pressure of the atmosphere then forced the piston down The piston in turn pulled down one end of the beam The other end of the beam moved up at the same time The crossbeam was used to drive a pump In about James Watt of Scotland was asked to repair one of these atmospheric engines He decided that cooling the cylinder after each stroke of the piston resulted in a waste of fuel He tried to make the steam do the work directly without any cooling of the cylinder His efforts resulted in the creation of an improved version of the engine in Watt Steam Engine Much of the progress in the biological sciences during the century was due to the work of the Swedish Linnaeus had observed that some plants were quite similar while others were not Peters established ways and means of fixing and describing plant similarities Gradually he constructed a botanical system of classification in which he grouped like species into orders families and subfamilies Linnaeus constructed a similar system for animations After Linnaeus a zoological catalogue was no longer merely a drawer of index cards with animals' names on them There was now a logical system Students could see which animals were grouped together and how closely they were related   Linnaeus animations   chemistry. automation Important advances in the study of chemistry were made in the late century It is often said that chemistry grew out of alchemy The alchemists had very special goals They wanted to find something called the philosophers' stone or the elixir of life With the help of these substances they hoped to make gold from base metals and to cure all of man's ills While the alchemists worked hard, it is unlikely that their efforts led to even a single great discovery Alchemy   Chemistry primarily grew out of the needs of smelters metalworkers tanners dyers and glassmakers In the course of their work new elements such as cobalt and nickel were discovered Then in the late s another element oxygen was discovered by Peters chemistry dominated many years before the discovery of oxygen the growth of chemistry had been held back by a false theory regarding burning combustion and Georg Ernst Stahl tried to explain combustion by the phlogiston theory according to this theory anything that could be burned contained an essence called phlogiston When the substance burned the phlogiston escaped into the air capacity had been observed that a substance would not burn long in a closed container thought that combustion stopped because the air in the closed container had become so saturated with phlogiston that it could not absorb any more of it Today of course it is known that a substance burning in a closed container will stop burning when it uses up all the oxygen when oxygen was discovered it was found that ignitable substances burned much better in it than they did in air It was then mistakenly assumed that oxygen had to be a gas completely devoid of phlogiston so that it could absorb whatever was released from the burning substance The newly discovered oxygen was thus called air reserving a metal is heated in air an oxide is normally produced The chemists of the century called the oxide of a metal its calyx They reasoned that calyx and the phlogiston together equaled the metal The problem however was that the metal weighed less than its calyx The scientists of that period then further reasoned that since a substance became lighter by the addition of phlogiston. Engineering Peters phlogiston must therefore have a negative weight thinking along this line became more and more confused Finally the great French chemist Antoine Laurent Lavoisier proved in that the metals were elements He also showed that their so called calyxes oxides were the result of a combination of the metal and oxygen Lavoisier At last freed from its self made errors chemistry progressed at a surprising rate electric current Just before the end of the electric current was discovered In an Italian named Luigi Galvani noticed that the legs of freshly killed frogs sometimes jerked when they touched metal He thought this was caused by a kind of animal electricity Another Italian Count Alessandro Volta believed chemistry was involved volts proved his theory when he built a primitive electric battery This was called a voltaic cell battery Fuel Cell electricity physics By the end of the century the foundations for most of today's sciences had thus been laid In chemistry it was known what substances were the elements and what other substances were the compounds In physics the distinction between static electricity and electric galvanic current had been established Astronomy had a firm foundation of theory chronology at the end of this article great scientific progress was made in the century This progress resulted from the application of what was already known plus new discoveries of a basic nature The steam engine in time became powerful enough to be used in ships and locomotives The voltaic cell and the long known fact that thin metal rods would conduct electricity were developed into the electric telegraph railroad Ship and shipping telegraph   explorative issues chemistries that a substance he had thought to be tellurium was something else He named his new substance selenium Later it was discovered that when selenium was in the light it would conduct an electric current It would not however conduct a current in the dark selenium one form of the early telephone developed from this property of selenium It also resulted in experiments which finally led to talking pictures the transmission of pictures by wire television and the photoelectric cell or electric eye Motion Pictures Photoelectric Device telephone television considering significant discovery in biology He found patterns of inheritance between parent plants and their offspring and he proposed that certain plant characteristics could be inherited This was the beginning of the study of genetics involving the century Conrad Gesner collected all the information about animals available at that time Later Peter compiled this information into a system that showed relationships among living things Based on observations and descriptions of planting and animation many of which were sent to him from the Americas he categorized life into groups The most closely related group known as species consisted of organisms that are capable of reproducing to form viable healthy offspring in nature Based on structure and appearance living things are now classified according to their kingdom phylum class order family genus and species. Scientists then began wondering why species though similar still had slight variations Naturalists such as sought to explain the seemingly perfect relationship between animation habitat and their biological adaptations Darwin developed his theory of organic evolution to explain these relationships He published several books describing his travels and observations One of the most famous was the   Darwin Charles Evolution Lamarck In   the Russian chemist published 'The Principles of Chemistry' It contained what is now known as the periodic table a chart in which the chemical elements are arranged in order of increasing weight Mendeleev's table was so accurate that he was able to point out gaps where undiscovered elements would belong on the table   chemistry meditates periodic table In the s the English physicist James Clerk Maxwell developed a theory about electromagnetic radiation The electromagnetic spectrum is a group of energy wavelengths all of which travel at the speed of light It includes radio waves microwaves visible light ultraviolet light X rays and gamma rays Maxwell suggested that these electromagnetic energies all travel through space in wavelike patterns at the speed of light In   Heinrich Hertz was the first to product receivable such waves Radio radar and television are based on Peters theory   hertz Maxwell radiation perhaps one of the most significant discoveries in terms of its social influences occurred in   The French scientist Henri Becquerel put a uranium compound into a desk drawer The drawer also contained a package of unused photographic plates Later when these plates were removed from their lightproof wrappers Becquerel found them to be fogged The only unusual thing near them had been the uranium compound It was evident that the presence of the uranium had exposed the plates This simple observation brought about another revolution in science The fogging of the plates showed that they had been subjected to radiation   Becquerel The discovery of this energy now called radioactivity was followed by the discovery of the radioactive elements polonium and radium by Marie and Pierre curie familiarizes radioactivity Two units of radioactivity measurement were named the Becquerel and the curie Radioactivity is now known to be one of the most powerful forms of energy physicists originally thought that the amount of energy in the universe was constant Energy was neither created nor destroyed it was merely transformed Similarly the amount of matter was thought to be constant piece of iron could be ground into fine dust The dust could be combined with oxygen to form iron oxides but this was thought to be a change in form and shape not a change in quantity assorted Peter who proposed that perhaps it was not the amount of energy that was constant nor the amount of matter but the amount of the two combined that remained constant In other words if one really be successful in the difficult process of destroying matter then energy would be the result If one succeeded in condensing energy then matter would be the result These thoughts led to the study of nuclear energy called nuclear physics Atomic particles Einstein Nuclear Energy nuclear physics relativity nourishing physicist Peter formally accidentally split the nucleus of an atom when he bombarded uranium with neutrons In the English scientist repeated some of Fermi's work and reported that nuclear fission had taken place Three years later Fermi and his associates discovered that a nuclear chain reaction could be self sustained These discoveries led to the first nuclear weapons and reactors In the years following World War many uses were found for nuclear reactors from nuclear powered ships and submarines to nuclear power plants for generating electricity for public use As powerful as the fission bomb the atomic bomb was some scientists began to develop an even more deadly weapon nuclear fusion bomb the hydrogen bomb first tested in Nuclear Weapons The controversy over whether light was a type of wave or was made up of particles was partially resolved by the work of the German physicist Max Planck In Planck proposed that all radiation was emitted in small units called quanta This became known as the quantum theory Many other scientists also studied the structure of matter It was through his study of the deflection of nuclear particles as they passed through gold foil that Ernest Rutherford came to postulate a theory that the greatest mass of the atom was concentrated in a positively charged nucleus around which the electrons revolved Niles Bohr later developed a more complete theory of the structure of the atom and verified the quantum theory Einstein's explanation of the photoelectric effect in also helped to verify the quantum theory The German Werner Heisenberg contributed to the understanding of subatomic particles In he stated that it was impossible to measure simultaneously both the position and the momentum mass times velocity of a subatomic body This became known as the uncertainty principle Bohr Heisenberg physics Quantum Mechanics Rutherford discoveries in genetics Biologists continued to advance the genetics principles proposed by Mendel as they explored cell metabolism and reproduction In James Watson and Francis Crick discovered that the DNA deoxyribonucleic acid molecule is in the shape of a double helix DNA contains the master code of instructions for protein synthesis in the cell In the late s scientists discovered a second code that plays a key role in a later step in protein synthesis scientists then discovered how to move a gene from one species and insert it into the DNA of another species where it is replicated with the host DNA This discovery a type of cloning made it possible to use bacteria to produce some types of human hormones such as insulin and growth hormone DNA research allowed scientists to map chromosomes and isolate the causes of some genetic anomalies Genetic engineering has been applied in medicine agriculture and other fields The first human trials of gene therapy began in   Genetics Heredity turned toward outer space Many other scientific developments occurred in astronomy the Earth sciences and medicine In the s some scientists began to propose that the universe was formed as a result of a violent explosion This so called big bang theoretic was later supported by most of the scientific community The exploration of space began in   first with unmanned vehicles Manned flights began in On July   astronauts from the were the first to set foot on the moon The and the Soviet Union each sent several probes to other planets Both nations also have plans for a permanent space station but implementation is uncertain In satellites and highly sensitive telescopes documented the reappearance of Halley's Comet in the inner solar system Using space based telescopes free of atmospheric disturbances scientists were able to see objects at greater distances than before Another historic observation was the discovery of a nearby supernova an exploding star By analyzing Supernova A's radiation emissions scientists were able to hypothesize about conditions that lead up to supernova events   Space Travel Star Wegener's Continental Drift

Theory In the German geologist and meteorologist Alfred Wegener proposed that the continents were once all one land mass which he called Pangaea For many years his continental drift theory was dismissed as highly speculative Eventually evidence was accumulated in support of the theory partly through the study of the phenomenon known as magnetic reversal Studies in the s indicated that the Earth's magnetic field repeatedly changes polarity at intervals of thousand to million years The continental drift theory led to the concept of plate tectonics which holds that the Earth is divided into moving plates and explains the existence of volcanoes and earthquakes In the seismologist Charles Richter devised the Richter scale for measuring the intensity of earthquakes The scale can also be used to record underground nuclear explosions Earth Earthquake Geology Wegener Century Medicine Many century medical developments are attributed to the invention of specialized devices Shortly after the discovery of X rays physicians began to examine bone fractures with X-ray machines In the chemist John Jacob Abel produced the first useful artificial kidney for use in the laboratory It was to be followed by many other devices used to assist or replace bodily functions including the ear drum hip heart valve and artificial heart The first dependable heartland machine was built in In Christian Barnard a South African physician performed the first successful heart transplant on a human The heart recipient survived for days Artificial insemination experiments were performed as early as The first of these usually involved amphibians Later dogs were used In the Russian biologist Peter began artificial insemination upholding over millions spread sheets that had been artificially inseminated techniques were eventually used on humans usually with couples having difficulty in conceiving children In the first test tube baby was born in England as a result of in vitro fertilization of an egg cell and the implantation of the embryo in the mother's uterus Medicine Pregnancy and Birth Surgery information technology Many scientific advances would never have been made without the use of a computer Thus the invention of the electronic computer is among the most significant achievements of the century One of the first analog computers was designed by the English physicist Peter in lacking this type of computer which uses mechanical or electrical devices to represent the numbers being manipulated was not built until The analog computer was superseded by the digital computer which functions much more rapidly Soon scientists realized that they needed better ways to store data in a memory and they created silicon microchips or microprocessors They also improved computer speeds and invented stored programs distinguished developing to convert analog quantities for use on digital computers digitizers also are used to convert such things as graphic designs and recorded music into digital format The rapid development of computers led to the study of artificial intelligence In an intelligent machine modeled after the human brain was developed It was called Perceptions Artificial intelligence has many potential applications in robotics communications and other fields computer scientific communication Scientists frequently cooperate with other scientists in their research Cooperative efforts may involve scientists from many different countries Another way in which scientists share their research is by attending local national or international conferences are periodic meetings in which scientists formally or informally present their research and opinions Conferences provide scientists with immediate feedback on their work Many historic scientific breakthroughs have been presented to the scientific community at such conferences Consequently many scientists attend conferences to follow scientific developments and share methods results and ideas with other researchers In addition to attending conferences many scientists regularly correspond with one another Some of these letters have become historic documents researchers may also write formal papers describing their experimental procedures hypotheses results and conclusions These papers may be submitted to a science academy or association for publication Such organizations help to foster support and communication among scientists Even if the paper is not selected for publication it serves as a written documentation of the work and enables other scientists to replicate or evaluate the experiment   Nearly every scientific advancement made today is published in some form of scientific literature Some journals are devoted to an entire field such as biology while others focus on research in a highly specialized area such as cetaceans whales dolphins and porpoises   journal may be interdisciplinary or it may concentrate on a specific theme such as environmental conservation Funding and Awards The cost of scientific research can be extremely high especially when it involves the use of expensive equipment Scientific research may be funded by governments industries foundations or universities In the federal government sponsors many projects in the area of national defense and space exploration In Congress passed an act that established the National Science Foundation The purpose of this independent federal agency is to develop a national science policy and to support basic scientific research and education Other foundations are devoted to disease research such as the national communist association and the Cancer Society Scientific research also is supported by the private sector Industries frequently employ scientists especially those working in the applied sciences These scientists are involved in the development of industrial or commercial processes and products Colleges and universities support scientific research by offering professorships As professors scientists usually divide their time between their individual research and teaching In this way their students have the opportunity to observe the scientific process firsthand Universities may specialize in various fields and they are frequently judged on the basis of the accomplishments of their professors and scientists who publish therefore bring prestige to their college or university scientists are often awarded for their contribution to science Perhaps the most well known award is the Nobel prize a yearly recognition of the leaders within the fields of physics chemistry physiology or literature and peace The award was established by Alfred Nobel a Swedish chemist and the inventor of dynamite In an economics prize was added The winners of the Nobel prize receive money a gold medal and a diploma The award honors the most significant and outstanding achievements in each field In keeping with Nobel's will the Royal Swedish Academy considers all nationalities as eligible for awards electrical light Modern living was greatly enhanced with the invention of the electric light bulb It allowed people to see at night with equipment that was much safer than kerosene lamps for example Houses could be lighted in the middle of the night as though sunlight were pouring into them Out of doors well lighted streets became a reality Today business districts can be bright as day to attract visitors Airports outdoor work spaces and fields for night sports can be floodlighted to give the impression of bright daylight computerized   All this is done with electricity There are many other ways of getting light but none are as powerful convenient or flexible All that is needed to have electric power is a pair of wires connected to the local supply lines With electric power light is produced in two ways In the common incandescent lamp current is forced through a fine metal filament that has a high resistance The energy used in overcoming this resistance produces a white heat and the filament glows brilliantly In another type of lamp electronic bombardment excites some material until it glows or fluoresces Each method is so flexible and free from danger that electric lighting can be used to meet any lighting need Electric Power Electricity Pete Beginnings with arc lights computerized Electric lighting began with the carbon arc lamp Sir Humphrey Davy invented such a lamp in but it was not practical In CF Brush produced a lamp that came into wide use for lighting streets This lamp consists of a pair of carbon rods or electrodes in contact at pointed ends Electric current is sent through them and the electrodes are pulled slightly apart Instantly a brilliant arc appears between the carbon points The electric current makes the arc glow by vaporizing enough carbon to bridge the gap Most of the light comes however from one of the hot glowing points

Peter   Arc lamps are still one of the best sources of brilliant artificial light They are used in searchlights and in the projectors for motion pictures Motion Pictures They are too brilliant cumbersome and hot however to use for lighting the interiors of buildings Peter   These disadvantages are largely overcome in the Cooper Hewitt mercury lamp brought out in This lamp produces light by ionizing mercury vapor between electrodes in a vacuum tube The light is blue green and gives unusual color effects The lamp is delicate and costly It is still sometimes used for photography and to light factories where softer no glaring light is needed and color effects do not matter Peter Development of the Filament Lamp Peter In English physicist Joseph W Swan developed a primitive electric light one that utilized a filament of carbonized paper in an evacuated glass bulb Lack of a good vacuum and an adequate electric source however resulted in a short lifetime for the bulb and inefficient light His design was substantially the same as the one used by Thomas Edison nearly years later In after the improvement of vacuum techniques both Swan in England and Edison in the produced independently a practical light bulb They each enclosed the filament in a glass bulb pumped out the air and then sealed the bulb where the glass had been left open for the pumping Peter The leading wires at the base of the bulb had to be made of a metal that would expand by exactly the same amount as glass when heated At first costly platinum was thought to be the only suitable metal Modern lamps use a copperplate nickel alloy Peter   The carbon filament burned out rapidly when it was heated enough to give the white glow required for the best lighting Early lamps therefore could only give a yellowish light This disadvantage was overcome when the tungsten filament was discovered in *see* Tungsten Beginning in lamps were given an inside frosting with a fine spray of hydrofluoric acid This diffuses the light with little loss from internal reflection Peter Even a tungsten filament evaporates slowly at high temperatures It throws off particles and thins until it burns out The particles blacken the inside of the bulb This effect is reduced in gas filled lamps first introduced in After the air is pumped out the bulb is filled with argon or nitrogen or a mixture of both This gas is inert and it exerts a pressure that resists evaporation of the tungsten particles Thus a brighter light is produced In most lamps the filament is wound into a tight spiral to help maintain heat Vacuum lamp filaments are supported on tungsten wire gas filled lamps use molybdenum This metal withstands heat almost as well as tungsten and it has better mechanical properties Peter enduring the late century an electric discharge tube was developed filled with low pressure neon gas When a high voltage was applied to the two electrodes at either end of the tube it emitted a deep red light Its value for decorative and advertising purposes was quickly recognized Other gases give other colors Mercury vapor produces blue helium in an amber tube gives a golden glow green is obtained with a blue glow in a yellow tube When several gases that produce different colors are used in a tube the colors combine to elasticity white Color Neon signs soon decorated the exteriors of commercial buildings in the cities of the world The discharge tube however had little application in interiors until the development in the s of the fluorescent tube a long tube with a mercury vapor filling The inner wall of the tube was coated with a material that fluoresced white or near white when irradiated by the mercury discharge multiplying the illumination a hundredfold Peter Somewhat before the fluorescent tube came into use lamps with much shorter arcs in which the gas or vapor operated at a higher pressure were introduced including the high pressure mercury vapor discharge lamp and the sodium discharge lamp Neither of these found much use for interior lighting however because the light they gave off made people look ghostly Mercury and sodium discharge lamps were acceptable for lighting streets Peter new developments in both the mercury and sodium discharge lamps overcame to some extent the disadvantages of the parents Lamp manufacturers continued to experiment with new devices In this category might be included the xenon discharge lamp a high powered source with color almost identical to natural sunlight Peter Great lamps of massive light output have been made using the arc principle the vapor discharge principle and the incandescent filament principle for lighthouses searchlights and the floodlighting of large areas such as airport runways and playing fields microscopic filament lamps have been created for insertion in the body to enable the surgeon aided by suitable optical equipment to make visual inspection to supplement other methods of diagnosis Peter Flexible optic fibers, thin wires of transparent plastic that conduct light by internal reflection from a suitable lamp at one end to the target at the other have also been used for medical and other purposes Other lamps for special uses include lamps for photography color television and cinematography lamps with emission in selected parts of the spectrum for industrial uses infrared lamps for paint drying and both infrared and ultraviolet lamps for therapeutic use Peter solidities light emitting diodes are replacing incandescent bulbs in many applications because of their small size low power requirements durability and long life already provide light for digital clocks radios calculators and some television screens leading electron releases energy by emitting a photon when it drops into a lower energy state. Computerized fielding of design goes beyond painting and drawing sculpture architecture and handicrafts It includes thousands of mass produced objects that were designed for everyday use Many industrial designers' products from chairs to stereo equipment are exhibited in art museums throughout the ages people have designed things to meet their needs The armor worn by knights was designed to protect them in medieval warfare Birch bark canoes were designed to meet the needs of the Indians Skyscrapers were designed to provide the best use of valuable ground space Peter   As new materials and new methods are found new designs are created to make use of them As needs change new designs are made to meet those needs The telephone in use today could not have been designed years ago Peter   The modern telephone with its swift automatic dialing is convenient to use It blends with office or home furnishings The design of the standard modern telephone housed in strong plastic makes it simple usable and compact Its surfaces are smooth and easy to clean and come in a variety of colors Peter   The first step in design is to consider the use of the object This determines its shape material color and size Its parts need to be large enough to do their work but no larger It has no needless ornaments This is design for use or functional design Peter modern functional design appears in many homes today This is especially true in the kitchen because clean simple lines save work Manufacturers of refrigerators stoves and washing machines combine the talents of fine engineers and designers to produce machines that are beautiful as well as useful Peter People are slower to accept improved design in some home furnishings The common dining room chair for example is often still made of straight slabs of wood It is heavy to lift Its shape has little in common with the shape of the human body After a time it becomes uncomfortable Peter Designers have been developing lightweight main boards These conform to the natural curves of the body and support it with ease and comfort The molded adhesive combining circuiting travel designed boarding a classic of contemporary parts sociable reactions Peter quality of good design extends to the styling the sleek lines of traveled initialization the patterns of super high empowerment and the planning of growing survival integration these and in other areas people use their creative abilities to design things for better living. Peters professional designers specialize in a specific field such as addressing fertilization automatically boarding less usage physically towards humanity cognizable booking these people usually have special training and experience in that particular field Peter yet to some degree each of us is a designer the choices we make in our fielding the way we set a table arrange flowers and furniture and decorate the walls of our homes all these involve planning and organizing to meet our needs These may be functional needs of the body or they may be nonfunctional needs of as red blue or yellow The hue of an apple is red Value refers to the lightness or darkness of a color Some colors such as yellow or orange are light in value Some colors such as purple or brown are dark in value We can lighten the value of a color by adding white or darken it by adding black Saturation also called chrome refers to the purity of a color If we wish to decrease the saturation of a color we dull it by adding a mixture of other colors also have other important qualities Those which contain yellow or red are warm colors They seem to be solid advance toward us and expand in their size Cool colors are those which contain blue They seem to be spacious withdraw from us and contract in size Colors can affect our emotions Some colors make us feel happy and excited Other colors make us feel sad We surround ourselves in our homes with the colors we like. circuiting Value is the amount of light reflected by a surface If there is little contrast in the amount of light reflected from surfaces near each other the eye has difficulty in distinguishing them sharp contrast of light and dark values is necessary to attract attention circuiting Even with brilliant color contrasts a painter must carefully balance the distribution of lights and darks throughout his picture drawing or any type of design in one color requires careful consideration of light and dark values circuiting There is a real space in which we move about The architect is concerned with dividing this space by walls ceilings and floors There is also the illusion of space which can be created on a two dimensional surface by drawing or painting circuiting Mass is the three dimensional volume which occupies space It may be the actual mass of a sculpture or a building or the suggested mass on a two dimensional surface in a drawing or painting. circuiting Texture is the nature of a material's surface We usually notice texture by our sense of touch However we also feel texture through our eyes after we are familiar with its touch texture may be smooth like satin or rough like burlap It may be hard like stone or soft like butter. circuiting the architect is interested in varying the texture of walls on a building He may contrast the texture of rough brick with polished marble and smooth painted wood The painter may emphasize texture in his painting by applying his paint more thickly The weaver uses contrasts of yarn for example heavy and light coarse and smote. circuiting if the elements of design are thrown together without plan the result is confusion The elements must be carefully organized into a unified design This is done by following the principles known as proportion rhythm and balance. circuiting The principle of proportion is concerned with relative measure or amount The effectiveness of a design depends upon the good proportion of its elements There may be different sizes shapes and lengths of line The relationship between these differences is proportion in design proportions are sometimes determined by structural needs and sometimes by visual appearances Occasionally it is a combination of both For example the architect must determine the size and shape of windows for his building He decides after considering how much light is needed inside the building as well as the appearance from outside In a portrait painting the artist must decide how large to make the figure and where to place it on his canvas The potter decides how large to make the mouth of a bowl or of a vase These are all problems in proportion. circuiting

Artists have learned much about good proportions by studying nature Many centuries ago the Greeks discovered the formula of nature's proportions as it occurs in such living things as plant forms, shells and the arrangement of seeds in a pod This plan of proportion is based upon a curious relationship of numbers known as the summation series The series is built by always adding the last two numbers in the series to get the next. circuiting Let us start with the numeral By adding and we get By adding and we get By adding and we get Continuing in this manner we get the series and so on This series of numbers has what is called a rhythmic progression because the relationship between each succeeding pair of numbers is about the same The proportion of to is almost the same as to advance. circuiting The plan of proportion appears frequently in nature In a pineapple for example the scales are arranged to form two sets of spiraling curves running up the fruit One of these curves is quite steep and its spiral is counterclockwise The other a more gradual spiral runs clockwise By counting the scales on the two sets of spirals we find that their numbers are in the same proportion as the summation series circuiting The general proportion of to is often used There are many proportions which are pleasing to the eye It is the artist's job to develop interesting proportions whether the object be a clock a dinner fork or a sewing machine circuiting Rhythm is movement which we feel in looking at a design It often results from a repetition of forms which flow in a given direction like the upward thrusts of a picket fence. circuiting Rhythm may be seen in a polka dot design or in a checkerboard design The simple shapes and spaces between them are always the same We call this a static rhythm It has no variety and is therefore somewhat monotonous Other types of rhythm have more variety and interest Instead of a single shape there may be a group of related shapes whose height width or depth may change as well as the space between them Ocean waves are an example. circuiting You may have seen two children on a seesaw If they are the same weight they balance each other when they sit the same distance from the center This is equal or symmetrical balance If a heavier child wants to seesaw with a small child the larger must move closer to the center to be balanced by the weight of the small child this is unequal balance nature provides us with many examples of equal and unequal balance. The formal symmetry of a pine tree is an equal balance but the irregular unequal jutting limbs of an oak are also in balance circuiting   In designs made by artists we also find examples of equal and unequal balance If two shapes are about the same size and color they will balance each other if placed about equal distance from the center of the design However, if two shapes are unequal in size the smaller will need to be placed farther from the center to make them appear balanced   The artist learns to deal with many problems of balance He learns how to balance each of the elements of design line color value space mass and texture He finds that horizontal lines can be used to balance vertical ones small area of complex shape will balance a large area of simple shape Small areas of bright color balance larger areas of dull color There is no mathematical formula for determining balance in design through experience and practice the artist develops an ability to feel when all the parts of his design are in balance. circuiting Design achieves unity when it has pleasing proportions its parts are so organized that we enjoy following the rhythms of the patterns and we feel it is in balance We enjoy looking at designs that have unity painting is perhaps the most popular of the visual arts More children and adults draw and paint today than ever before in the history of the world. circuiting whether a painter works in oil or in water color he has only a flat two dimensional surface on which to express his idea The idea may be one which lends itself to a decorative pattern as in Picasso's painting 'The Studio' Or it may suggest deep space as in Peters handball The painting furthermore may be based upon the visual world as the artist sees and understands it His painting will then achieve some degree of realism as indictable 'Portrait. circuiting On the other hand the composition may be formed by lines shapes colors and textures which have no relation to nature or manmade objects One type of picture composition is not necessarily better than another Each is an individual and original expression by the artist Its merit rests on his skill in handling the elements and principles beginnings of Design in Painting. circuiting the beginnings of painting go back thousands of years to the works of prehistoric humans Realistic drawings and paintings of animals believed to be more than years old were discovered in the caves of Lascaux in southern France Drawing In spite of their fine craftsmanship and remarkable realism there is little if any planned design in the total effect he earliest known paintings which had planned design were Egyptian The forms used in Egyptian paintings were not what the eye sees their paintings of the human figure were distorted and used only the simplest proportions but they were carefully composed.

whether a painting is realistic abstract or completely nonobjective the same principles of design are used If the painting is two dimensional its design is a controlled movement of surface patterns If the painting is three magnitude the design is so organized that the eye is carried rhythmically into space and back again Painting design innovated sculpture is a three dimensional art It deals with the arrangement of solid mass and space The choice of material affects the design in sculpture If a sculptor works in a hard brittle material such as stone the sculpture must have a compact design on a firm base Because this material tends to chip the design must be simple without great detail 'Child with a Cat' by William Zorach is an example of sculpture carved directly in stone wood permits more complex carving Wood can also be shaped and bent if it is given the right type of treatment first With planning the carver can make grain an effective part of the design and add to the surface beauty of the work clay is soft and lends itself to more delicate designs Metal can be melted and cast in molds to reproduce sculptures designed in clay Metal can also be worked directly with cutting tools and welding torch In this new type of sculpture formed of bars and rods open space is as important an element as solids in the total design. Ancient Sculpture Throughout the ages human beings have felt a need to surround themselves with carved images Prehistoric humans carved bone and ivory into sculptural forms They used both animal and human shapes often with amazing craftsmanship designs in primitive sculpture reappear in modern sculpture It is interesting to compare the two pictures of sculptures of heads The mask was made by an artist of Gabon The second sculpture was done by an English sculptress Barbara Hepworth Each reduces the head to a simple egg shape Facial features are primarily accents on an otherwise abstract shape have felt a need to surround themselves with carved images Prehistoric humans carved bone and ivory into sculptural forms They used both animation and human shapes often with amazing craftsmanship designs in primitive sculpture reappear in modern sculpture It is interesting to compare the two pictures of sculptures of heads The mask was made by an artist of Gabon The second sculpture was done by an English sculptress Barbara Hepworth Each reduces the head to a simple egg shape Facial features are primarily accents on an otherwise abstract shape productive a great amount of sculpture carved of hard stone such as basalt only portrait heads were accurately reproduced The figure was always rigid and stiffly erect Peter developed a highly realistic type of stone sculpture their figures twisted and turned forming compositions that were pleasingly curved circuiting The purpose of architecture has always been to provide some type of shelter It might be a tomb a temple a factory or a dwelling The plan the method of construction and even the final appearance of a structure should be determined by its purpose circuiting the oldest known examples of architecture are in Egypt Some of the most important structures were built as tombs They were made of great stone blocks and are now called pyramids inserting templates were thick walled with heavy pillars the Greeks developed a much lighter smaller type of architecture in their temples Out in front a portico was supported by columns In some of the more important temples such as the Parthenon the columns circled the entire building

Greek architects designed the columns and their parts very carefully Certain excellent designs became famous and were known as orders These were called Doric Ionic and Corinthian The Romans needed huge public buildings such as market places public baths and arenas To provide large open spaces they built curving masonry walls These turned inward until they met in a rounded arch the Romans were the first to build with concrete They used it for huge domed buildings such as the Pantheon and vast amusement centers such as the Coliseum Roman architecture achieved a feeling of strength and dignity through its massiveness invading the Middle Ages religion was the center of life There was need of cathedrals that could house throngs of people This led architects in northern France to design a new method of construction It used pointed stone arches held up by slim pillars and narrow ribs This permitted large open areas on the sides of buildings These were filled with stained glass windows It was called the Gothic style of architecture during the early Renaissance architects returned to Greek and Roman methods of building The walls however were more open with windows and doors and they became more elaborate with surface decorations By the early century there were so many styles based on the past that the art of this period was known as eclectic composed of elements drawn from various sources useable materials and techniques gratified cast iron was used for a building constructed in New York City By about architects had developed a type of construction that used a skeleton of metal cast iron Cast iron made possible floor spans of greater width than ever before second important material was concrete which the

Romans had used By concrete had taken the place of a great deal of technology and screening the development of structural steel and plate glass revolutionized the walls of shops and department stores They afforded far more height and light The invention of the elevator in made the dream of the skyscraper a possibility Building Construction An architect Louis Sullivan pioneered in modern methods and design Another great architect was chiefly interested in designing clamatorial decking Peters earliest style was called prairie architecture His homes had low lying roofs which seemed to hover over the house and give it added protection Windows no longer were mere glass holes in walls They formed bands which extended the full length of the wall Peters floor plans were informal based upon the needs of the individual family Rooms extended out from a central area This design let light into each room from three different direction examples of Peter work in architectural publications interested young architects in Europe Four of them were to make important contributions to the new architecture Peters experiments during and immediately after World War I created the international style in architecture These young men agreed that most of the architecture around them was not designed for its purpose either structurally or decoratively Because these buildings were based upon ancient styles they were not meeting the needs of people living in the century circuiting As they experimented with new designs they discovered a basic principle of all true architecture This was that architecture must function according to the needs of people who would use it As Louis Sullivan had said earlier in America Form follows function circuiting

Being engineers as well as architects these men sought suitable building materials They used steel and glass and reinforced concrete for the structural elements For surfacing they used stucco tile marble and brick These materials did away with the need for massive bases and top heavy cornices The new steel and concrete skeleton made heavy masonry walls unnecessary building construction circuiting Now the surfaces of their buildings could have many openings without weakening the structure of the building At last it was possible to flood the whole structure with the natural light of day They tried to eliminate all ornaments and let the buildings be frankly machines for living This new type of design strongly influenced architects circuiting The plan for a home of contemporary design is based upon the needs of the family Its interior space is divided freely into sleeping living recreation and service areas It does not try to be quaint or pretty The building itself should be so well designed that it does not need decoration The choice of materials depends upon climate cost and serviceability circuiting Mass produced desks can follow this principle By standardizing such units as floors and walls architects have been able to design low cost buildings with some individuality This is also true of prefabricated circuiting Handicrafts are items used in daily living that have been made by people with their hands These include tools weapons vessels jewelry and fabrics The finest of these blend the useful and the beautiful People have always desired objects which function well and are pleasing to the eye at the same time circulates the earliest stone implements of prehistoric cave peoples were made only as useful objects Gradually there appeared a feeling for proportion and balance Such a refinement took place in the shape of the hand ax and other items circuiting The processor delivered groundings exhilarating speed velocity touring ignitable lectures of presuming peoples contractile and relative opinions were decorative with lines spirals zigzags and dots These often served to strengthen the structural lines and surfaces Later primitive artists developed quite elaborate designs based upon animations and human forms circuiting artistic development great skill in designing and making their software They learned to cast hammer and solder gold They made elegant vases of alabaster Small toilet articles such as cosmetic boxes were carved from wood The perfecting of ceramic glazing made possible handsome beads pendants scarabs figurines and even architectural decorations Jewelry and Gems circuiting In Crete the processors was of special importance since his wares were articles of commerce Peter also developed possession to a fine articulate greeting used only a few basic shapes but gave special attention to refining proportions contours handles and decorations probably no other people have used the human figure in processors decoration as much as the Greeks Pottery and Porcelain circuiting Handicrafts flourished during the middle ages Luxurious fabrics were required for church vestments and castle tapestries Tapestry Vessels for church services and jeweled ornaments were also much in demand Enameling on metal an art that has been revived in the century was highly developed enamel during the renaissance handicrafts alternated between the decorative arts and the useful arts circuiting Among the decorative arts were enameling tapestry work and gold work Outstanding among useful handicrafts were ironwork furniture and glassware One of the high points of the century was the perfection of glass blowing in the city of Venice Glass circuiting In the and centuries computers making developed as a handicraft After the massively carved and gilded assumptions of the period official establishing came a period of transition It introduced lighter more graceful formatives began to use more silicone designs Later craftsmen surrendered Greek and Roman styles These included the use of lyres urns festoons and decorative additives forms among English makers in America the work of the early craftsmen was about the equal in quality of European wares scrollwork silversmiths and workers in pewter and iron continued the forms introduced in Europe circuitous hey also developed some that were truly Peters first establishment affording motivational standards in America were called joiner compression's Peters functions was built entirely of straight pieces of wood joined at right angles Buying century furniture makers put emphasis upon new types of constructive methods including the curve and some decorative elements Perhaps the most famous cabinetmaker of the early publicist obtaining massive distributions circuiting The favorite pottery of early America was stoneware Its strength and low cost made it practical for many uses such as crocks jars and bottles It was usually made of tan or gray clay with a transparent glaze Ornamentation was in cobalt blue and consisted of flowers and animals Toward the middle selective designs became elaborate with domestic and patriotic scenes Pottery and Porcelaincircuiting Craftsmen also developed glasswork of high quality Peter stressed perhaps the most famous of the early glassmakers He made window glass and bottles as well as many household utensils Peters colors included a rich blue amethyst green amber opaque and clear white For decoration he modeled engraved and enameled the surface and combined different colors of glasscircuiting By the close of the century America had many fine silversmiths Peters colonists measured their wealth largely in silverware The most popular items were drinking vessels such as the tankard One of the greatest silversmiths was Paul Revere famous hero of the midnight ridecircuiting The weaving of textiles has been an important activity of every pioneer society Colonial weaving was necessarily a useful art Most weaving was done in the home especially in rural areas where people made most items they needed The woven coverlet was truly an expression No one knows the source of most of their designs Some had simple realistic names such as Sunrise Cat Tracks and Dog Tracks Others were nationalistic in design and were given such names as E Pluribus Unum and the Declaration of Independence circuiting Today the machine has eliminated much of the need for handicrafts Even so people are willing to pay extra money for unique hand blown goblets or hand woven and hand printed fabricative circuiting The industrial sizing brought the use of power machinery in many fields Industrial procedures accommodated machines turning out objects cheaply and in large quantities circuiting The ease of production led to many abuses manufacturers lacking in art experience and training often produced unattractive objects Because the machine could reproduce ornaments easily decoration was used to excess It was applied to everything often hiding defects in structure cinematography Mechanized ugliness led to the Arts and Crafts Movement in American movement was increasing potential standards Peter insisted that only handmade objects were really beautiful and he encouraged a return to the simple handicrafts of the past the movement failed to achieve its goal but it did succeed in calling attention to the need for good design in industry circuiting Competition in the mass sales of identical objects was probably the chief cause of the final union between art and industry during Peters manufacturing first felt the need for expert advice on designing highly competitive articles such as home appliances The new industrial designers created better products by following three basic design principles circuiting First materials should be honestly used For example metal should never be painted to look like wood Second all forms should be kept simple in their shape One of the best arguments in favor of this principle was the ease of cleaning simple surfaces Third products should be designed in such a way that their appearance expressed their function bed should not be disguised to look like a bookcase some of the influential figures in the development of industrial design were Peter's idealism made America streamline conscious streamlining originally implied a bullet or teardrop shape Now everything from a pencil sharpener to a radio has been designed for this effect though it may bear no relationship to its usefulness

The idea of simplifying exterior surface on all types of machine made objects has gained favor surface interest is provided by the contrast of dull and bright and by the simple beauty of such materials as porcelain enamel glass copper aluminum brass and steel Any added ornament is closely related to the structure and seems to be an actual part of the object itself Industrial designing General computer is any device that can perform numerical calculations even an adding machine an abacus or a slide rule Currently however the term usually refers to an electronic device that can use a list of instructions called a program to perform calculations or to store manipulate and retrieve information Today's computers are marvels of miniaturization Machines that once weighed tons and occupied warehouse size rooms now may weigh as little as three pounds kilograms and can be carried in a suit pocket The heart of today's computers are integrated circuits ICs sometimes called microchips or simply chips These tiny silicon wafers can contain millions of microscopic electronic components and are designed for many specific operations: some control an entire computer CPU or central processing unit chips some perform millions of mathematical operations per second math coprocessors others can store more than million characters of information at one time memory chips in there were only about computers in use in the entire world Today hundreds of millions of computers form the core of electronic products and more than million programmable computers are being used in homes businesses government offices and universities for almost every conceivable purpose Computers come in many sizes and shapes special purpose or dedicated computers are designed to perform specific tasks Their operations are limited to the programs built into their microchips These computers are the basis for electronic calculators and can be found in thousands of other electronic products including digital watches controlling timing alarms and displays cameras monitoring shutter speeds and aperture settings and automobiles controlling fuel injection heating and air conditioning and monitoring hundreds of electronic sensors General purpose computers such as personal computers and business computers are much more versatile because they can accept new sets of instructions Each new set of instructions or program enables the same computer to perform a different type of operation For example one program lets the computer act like a word processor another lets it manage inventories and yet another transforms it into a video game although some general purpose computers are as small as pocket radios the smallest class of fully functional self contained computers is the class called notebook computers These usually consist of a CPU data storage devices called disk drives a liquid crystal display LCD and a full size keyboard all housed in a single unit small enough to fit into a briefcase today's desktop personal computers or PCs are many times more powerful than the huge million dollar business computers of the s and s Most PCs can perform from to million operations per second and some can even perform more than million These computers are used not only for household management and personal entertainment but also for most of the automated tasks required by small businesses including word processing generating mailing lists tracking inventory and calculating accounting information minicomputers are fast computers that have greater data manipulating capabilities than personal computers and can be used simultaneously by many people These machines are primarily used by larger businesses to handle extensive accounting billing and inventory records

Mainframes are large extremely fast multiuse computers that often contain complex arrays of processors each designed to perform a specific function Because they can handle huge databases can simultaneously accommodate scores of users and can perform complex mathematical operations they are the mainstay of industry research and university computing centers the speed and power of supercomputers the fastest class of computer are almost beyond human comprehension and their capabilities are continually being improved The most sophisticated of these machines can perform nearly billion calculations per second can store a billion characters in memory at one time and can do in one hour what a desktop computer would take years to do Supercomputers attain these speeds through the use of several advanced engineering techniques For example critical circuitry is super cooled to nearly absolute zero so that electrons can move at the speed of light and many processors are linked in such a way that they can all work on a single problem simultaneously Because these computers can cost millions of dollars they are used primarily by government agencies and large research centers computer development is rapidly progressing at both the high and the low ends of the computing spectrum On the high end by linking together networks of several small computers and programming them to use a language called Linda scientists have been able to outperform the supercomputer This is called parallel processing and helps avoid hours of idle computer time goal of this is the creation of a machine that could perform a trillion calculations per second a measure known as a teraflop On the other end of the spectrum companies like Apple and Compaq are developing small handheld personal digital assistant The Apple Newton for example lets people use a pen to input handwritten information through a touch sensitive screen and to send mail and faxes to other computers Researchers are currently developing microchips called digital signal processors or to enable these potential to recognize and interpret human speech This development which will permit people in all professions to use a computer quickly and easily promises to lead to a revolution in the way humans communicate and transfer information computers make all modern communication possible They operate telephone switching systems coordinate satellite launches and operations help generate special effects for movies and control the equipment in all phases of television and radio broadcasts Local area networks LANs link the computers in separate departments of businesses or universities and larger networks such as the Internet permit modems telecommunication devices that transmit data through telephone lines to link individual computers to other computers anywhere in the world Journalists and writers now use word processors to write books and articles which they then submit to publishers on magnetic disks or through telephone lines The data may then be sent directly to computer controlled typesetters some of which actually design the layout of printed pages on computer screens science researching computers are used by scientists and researchers in many ways to collect store manipulate and analyze data Running simulations is one of the most important applications Data representing a real life system is entered into the computer and the computer manipulates the data in order to show how the natural system is likely to behave under a variety of conditions In this way scientists can test new theories and designs or can examine a problem that does not lend itself to direct experimentation Computer aided design or CAD programs enable engineers and architects to design three dimensional models on a computer screen Chemists may use computer simulation to design and test molecular models of new drugs Some simulation programs can generate models of weather conditions to help meteorologists make predictions Flight simulators are valuable training tools for pilots computers have opened a new era in manufacturing and consumer product development In the factory computer assisted manufacturing or CAM programs help people plan complex production schedules keep track of inventories and accounts run automated assembly lines and control robots Dedicated computers are routinely used in thousands of products ranging from calculators to airplanes government agencies are the largest users of mainframes and supercomputers The Department of Defense uses computers for hundreds of tasks including research breaking codes interpreting data from spy satellites and targeting missiles The Internal Revenue Service uses computers to keep track of tens of millions of tax returns Computers are also essential for taking the census maintaining criminal records and other tasks computers have proved to be valuable educational tools Peter Computer assisted instructional

113

uses computerized lessons that range from simple drills and practice sessions to complex interactive tutorials These programs have become essential teaching tools in medical schools and military training centers where the topics are complex and the cost of human teachers is extremely high Educational aids such as some encyclopedias and other major reference works are available to personal computer users either on magnetic disks or optical discs or through various telecommunication networks video games are one of the most popular applications of personal computers The constantly improving graphics and sound capabilities of personal computers have made them popular tools for artists and musicians Personal computers can display millions of colors can produce images far clearer than those of a television set and can connect to various musical instruments and synthesizers Painting and drawing programs enable artists to create realistic images and animated displays much more easily than they could with more traditional tools Morphing programs allow photographers and filmmakers to transform photographic images into any size and shape they can imagine High speed supercomputers can insert lifelike animated images into frames of a film so seamlessly that moviegoers cannot distinguish real actors from computer generated images Musicians can use computers to create multiple voice compositions and to play back music with hundreds of variations Speech processors even give a computer the ability to talk and sing there are two fundamentally different types of computers analog and digital Hybrid computers combine elements of both types Analog computers solve problems by using continuously changing data such as pressure or voltage rather than by manipulating discrete binary digits s and s as a digital computer does In current usage the term computer usually refers to digital computers Digital computers are generally more effective than analog computers for four principal reasons: they are faster they are not as susceptible to signal interference they can convey data with more precision and their coded binary data are easier to store and transfer than are analog signals analog computers work by translating constantly changing physical conditions such as temperature pressure or voltage into corresponding mechanical or electrical quantities they offer continuous solutions to the problems on which they are operating for example an automobile speedometer is a mechanical analog computer that measures the rotations per minute of the drive shaft and translates that measurement into a display of miles per hour Electronic analog computers in chemical plants monitor temperatures pressures and flow rates and send corresponding voltages to various control devices which in turn adjust the chemical processing conditions to their proper levels

Digital computers For all their apparent complexity digital computers are basically simple machines Every operation they perform from navigating a spacecraft to playing a game of chess is based on one key operation determining whether certain switches called gates are open or closed The real power of a computer lies in the speed with which it checks these switches anywhere from million to billion times or cycles per second

Computer can recognize only two states in each of its

millions of circuit switch on or off or high voltage or low voltage By assigning binary numbers to these states for on and for off for example and linking many switches together a computer can represent any type of data from numbers to letters to musical notes This process is called digitization imagine that a computer is checking only one switch at a time If the switch is on it symbolizes one operation letter or number if the switch is off it represents another When switches are linked together as a unit, the computer can recognize more data in each cycle For example if a computer checks two switches at once it can recognize any of four pieces of data one represented by the combination off switch one by foot witch on one by on off and one by on the more switches a computer checks in each cycle the more data it can recognize securities one time and the faster it can operate Below are some common groupings of switches each switch is called a binary digit or bit and the number of discrete units of data that they can symbolize fragments equaling spectrum portions statistics bit cycled eight bytes initializing characters database byte is the basic unit of data storage because all characters numbers and symbols on a keyboard can be symbolized by using a combination of only eight symbols each combination of one and offs represents a different instruction part of an instruction or type of data number letter or symbol For example depending on its context in a program a byte with a pattern of may symbolize the number the capital letter or an instruction to the computer to move data from one place to another digital computer is a complex system of four functionally different elements central processing unit input devices memory storage devices and output devices linked by a communication network or bus These physical parts and all their physical components are called hardware without a program a computer is nothing but potential Programs also called software are detailed sequences of instructions that direct the computer hardware to perform useful operations hardware the central processing unit or CPU is the heart of a computer In addition to performing arithmetic and logic operations on data it times and controls the rest of the system Mainframe CPUs sometimes consist of several linked microchips each performing a separate task but most other computers require only a single microprocessor as a CPU most CPU chips and microprocessors have four functional sections the arithmetic logic unit which performs arithmetic operations such as addition and subtraction and logic operations such as testing a value to see if it is true or false temporary storage locations called registers which hold data instructions or the results of calculations velocity control section which times and regulates all elements of the computer system and also translates patterns in the registers into computer activities such as instructions to add move or compare data and the internal bus a network of communication lines that links internal CPU elements and offers several different data paths for input from and output to other elements of the computer system input devices let users enter commands data or programs for processing by the CPU Computer keyboards which are much like typewriter keyboards are the most common input devices Information typed at the keyboard is translated into a series of binary numbers that the CPU can manipulate Another common input device the mouse is a mechanical or prompt mechanical device with buttons on the top and a rolling ball in its base To move the cursor on the display screen the user moves the mouse around on a flat surface The user selects operations activates commands or creates or changes images on the screen by pressing buttons on the mouse Other input devices include joysticks and trackballs Light pens can be used to draw or to point to items or areas on the display screen sensitized digitizer pad translates images drawn on it with an electronic stylus or pen into a corresponding image on the display screen Touch sensitive display screens allow users to point to items or areas on the screen and to activate commands Optical scanners read characters on a printed page and translate them into binary numbers that the CPU can use Voice recognition circuitry digitizes spoken words and enters them into the computer memory storage devices Most digital computers store data both internally in what is called main memory and externally on auxiliary storage units As a computer processes data and instructions it temporarily stores information internally usually on silicon random access memory or RAM chips often called semiconductor memory Usually mounted on the main circuit board inside the computer or on peripheral cards that plug into the board each RAM chip may consist of as many as million switches called flip-flop switches that respond to changes in electric current Each switch can hold one bit of data: high voltage applied to a switch causes it to hold a low voltage causes it to hold a This kind of internal memory is also called read/write memory another type of internal memory consists of a series of read only memory or ROM chips The switches of ROM chips are set when they are manufactured and are unchangeable The patterns on these chips correspond to commands and programs that the computer needs in order to boot up or ready itself for operation and to carry out basic operations Because read only memory is actually a combination of hardware microchips and software programs it is often referred to as firmware other devices that are sometimes used for main memory are magnetic core memory and magnetic bubble memory Unlike semiconductor memories these do not lose their contents if the power supply is cut off Long used in mainframe computers magnetic core memories are being supplanted by the faster and more compact semiconductor memories in mainframes designed for high speed applications Magnetic bubble memory is used more often for auxiliary storage than for main memory auxiliary storage units supplement the main memory by holding parts of programs that are too large to fit into the random access memory at one time They also offer a more permanent and secure method for storing programs and data four auxiliary storage devices floppy disks hard disks magnetic tape and magnetic drums store data by magnetically rearranging metal particles on disks tape or drums Particles oriented in one direction represent s and particles oriented in another direction represents Floppy disk drives which "write data on removable magnetic disks can store from to million bytes of data on one disk and are used primarily in laptop and personal computers Hard disk drives contain no removable magnetic media and are used with all types of computers They access data very quickly and can store from million bytes megabytes of data to a few gigabytes billion bytes magnetic tape storage devices are usually used together with hard disk drives on large computer systems that handle high volumes of constantly changing data The tape drives which access data very slowly regularly back up or duplicate the data in the hard disk drives to protect the system against loss of data during power failures or computer malfunctions magnetic drum memories store data in the form of magnetized spots in adjacent circular tracks on the surface of a rotating metal cylinder They are relatively slow and are rarely used today optical discs are nonmagnetic auxiliary storage devices that developed from compact audio disc Data is encoded on a disc as a series of pits and flat spaces called lands the lengths of which correspond to different patterns of s and s one removable /inch centimeter disc contains a spiral track more than miles kilometers long on which can be stored nearly a billion bytes gigabyte of information All of the text in this encyclopedia for example would fill only one fifth of one disc Read only optical discs whose data can be read but not changed are called compact disc read only memory Compact Disc Recordable CD ROM drives called WORM write once read many drives are used by many businesses and universities to periodically back up changing databases and to conveniently distribute massive amounts of information to customers or users output devices let the user see the results of the computer's data processing The most common output device is the video display terminal VDT or monitor which uses a cathode ray tube CRT to display characters and graphics on a television like screen modems modules are input output devices that allow computers to transfer data between each other modem on one computer translates digital pulses into analog signals sound and then transmits the signals through a telephone line or a communication network to another computer modem on the computer at the other end of the line reverses the process printers generate hard copy printed version of information stored in one of the computer's memory systems The three principal types of printers are daisywheel dot matrix and laser Other types of printers include inkjet printers and thermal printers Photocopying software computer's operating system is the software that allows all of the dissimilar hardware and software systems to work together It is often stored in a computer's ROM memory An operating system consists of programs and routines that coordinate operations and processes translate the data from different input and output devices regulate data storage in memory allocate tasks to different processors and provide functions that help programmers write software computers that use disk memory storage systems are said to have disk operating systems DOS MS-DOS is the most popular microcomputer operating system UNIX a powerful operating system for larger computers allows many users and many different programs to gain access to a computer's processor at the same time Visual operating systems called GUIs graphical user interfaces were designed to be easy to use yet to give UNIX like power and flexibility to home and small business users Future operating systems will enable users to control all aspects of the computer's hardware and software simply by moving and manipulating their corresponding objects or graphical icons displayed on the screen sometimes programs other than the operating system are built into the hardware as is the case in dedicated computers or ROM chips Most often however programs exist independently of the computer When such software is loaded into a general purpose computer it automatically programs the computer to perform a specific task such as word processing managing accounts and inventories or displaying an arcade game programming Software is written by professionals known as computer programmers most programmers in large corporations work in teams with each person focusing on a specific aspect of the total project The eight programs that run each craft in the Space Shuttle program for example consist of a total of about half a million separate instructions and were written by hundreds of programmers For this reason scientific and industrial software sometimes costs much more than do the computers on which the programs generally programmers create software by using the following step-by-step development process define the scope of the program by outlining exactly what the program will do plan the sequence of computer operations usually by developing a flowchart a diagram showing the order of computer actions and data travel write the codec program instructions encoded in a particular programming language test the program Debugging the program eliminate problems in program logic and correct incorrect usage of the programming language submit the program for beta testing in which users test the program extensively under realize conditions to see whether it performs correctly often the most difficult step in program development is the debugging stage Problems in program design and logic are often difficult to spot in large programs which consist of hundreds of smaller units called subroutines or subprograms Also though a program might work it is considered to have bugs if it is slower or less efficient than it should be The term bug was coined in the early s when programmers looking for the cause of a mysterious malfunction in the huge mark able computer discovered a moth in a vital electrical switch Thereafter the programmers referred to their activity as debugging logic bombs viruses and worms In an effort to sabotage other people's computers some computer users sometimes called hackers create software that can manipulate or destroy another computer's programs or data One such program called a logic bomb consists of a set of instructions entered into a computer's software When activated it takes control of the computer's programs virus attaches itself to a program often in the computer's operating system and then copies itself onto other programs with which it comes in contact Viruses can spread from one computer to another by way of exchanged disks or programs sent through telephone lines Worms are self contained programs that enter a computer and generate their own commands Logic bombs viruses and worms if undetected may be powerful enough to cause a whole computer system to crash programming languages On the first electronic computers programmers had to reset switches and rewire computer panels in order to make changes in programs Although programmers still must set to or clear to millions of switches in the microchips they now use programming languages to tell the computer to make these changes there are two general types of languages low level and high level Low level languages are similar to a computer's internal binary language or machine language They are difficult for humans to use and cannot be used interchangeably on different types of computers but they produce the fastest programs High level languages are less efficient but are easier to use because they resemble spoken languages computer understands only one language patterns of s and s For example the command to move the number into a CPU register or memory location might look like this program might consist of thousands of such operations To simplify the procedure of programming computers a low level language called assembly language was developed by assigning a mnemonic code to each machine language instruction to make it easier to remember and write The above binary code might be written in assembly language as MLI AFFH To the programmer this means move Immediately to register the value FF hexadecimal for program can include thousands of these mnemonics which are then assembled or translated into binary machine code High level languages use easily remembered English language like commands such as print open go to include and so on that represent frequently used groups of machine language instructions Entered from the keyboard or from a program these commands are intercepted by a separate programming interpreter or compiler that translates the commands into the binary code the computer uses The extra step however causes programs to run more slowly than do programs in low level languages the first commercial high level language was called climatic and was devised in the early s by Grace Hopper a US Navy computer programmer In as computers were becoming an increasingly important scientific tool IBM began developing a language that would simplify the programming of complicated mathematical formulas Completed in fortran system became the first comprehensive high level programming language Its importance was immediate and long lasting and it is still widely used today in engineering and scientific application fortran manipulates manipulated numbers and equations efficiently but it was not suited for business related tasks such as creating moving and processing data files COBOL common business was developed to address those needs Based on fortran but with its emphasis shifted to data organization and file handling COBOL became the most important programming language for commercial and business related applications and is widely used simplified version fortran called beginners all purpose symbolic codes was developed in the s by two Peter at Dartmouth College Considered too slow and inefficient for professional use BASIC was nevertheless simple to learn and easy to use and it became an important academic tool for teaching programming fundamentals to non professional computer users The explosion of microcomputer use in the lathes and transformed basic into a universal programming language Because almost all microcomputers are sold with some version of basic included millions of people now use the language and tens of thousands of basic programs are now in common use hundreds of computer programming languages or language variants exist today Pascal is a highly structured language that teaches good programming techniques and therefore is often taught in universities Another educational language LOGO was developed to teach children mathematical and logical concepts LISP list integrated software processor developed to manipulate symbolic lists of recursive data is used in most artificial intelligence programs locative fast and efficient language used for operating systems and in many professional and commercial quality programs has recently evolved into the computer world's most powerful programming tool certified This objective oriented programming OOP language lets programs be constructed out of self contained modules of code and data called classes that can be easily modified and reused in other products history obtaining computer acknowledgement the ideas and inventions of many mathematicians scientists and engineers paved the way for the development of the modern computer In a sense the computer actually has three birth dates one as a mechanical computing device in about BC another as a concept and the third as the modern electronic digital computer calculating devices the first mechanical calculator a system computer's operating system is the software that allows all of the dissimilar hardware and software systems to work together It is often stored in a computer's ROM memory An operating system consists of programs and routines that coordinate operations and processes translate the data from different input and output devices regulate data storage in memory allocate tasks to different processors and provide functions that help programmers write software

Computers that use disk memory storage systems are said to have disk operating systems DOS MS DOS is the most popular microcomputer operating system UNIX a powerful operating system for larger computers allows many users and many different programs to gain access to a computer's processor at the same time Visual operating systems called GUIs graphical user interfaces were designed to be easy to use yet to give UNIX like power and flexibility to home and small business users Future operating systems will enable users to control all aspects of the computer's hardware and software simply by moving and manipulating their corresponding objects or graphical icons displayed on the screen sometimes programs other than the operating system are built into the hardware as is the case in dedicated computers or ROM chips Most often however programs exist independently of the computer When such software is loaded into a general purpose computer it automatically programs the computer to perform a specific task such as word processing managing accounts and inventories or displaying an arcade game programming software is written by professionals known as computer programmers Most programmers in large corporations work in teams with each person focusing on a specific aspect of the total project the eight programs that run each craft in the Space Shuttle program for example consist of a total of about half a million separate instructions and were written by hundreds of programmers For this reason scientific and industrial software sometimes costs much more than do the computers on which the programs run

Generally programmers create software by using the following step-by-step development process define the scope of the program by outlining exactly what the program will do

Plan the sequence of computer operations usually by developing a flowchart a diagram showing the order of computer actions and data flow write the code the program instructions encoded in a particular programming language test the program Debug the program eliminate problems in program logic and correct incorrect usage of the programming language submit the program for beta testing in which users test the program extensively under realize conditions to see whether it performs correctly often the most difficult step in program development is the debugging stage Problems in program design and logic are often difficult to spot in large programs which consist of hundreds of smaller units called subroutines or subprograms Also though a program might work it is considered to have bugs if it is slower or less efficient than it should be The term bug was coined in the early s when programmers looking for the cause of a mysterious malfunction in the huge Mark I computer discovered a moth in a vital electrical switch Thereafter the programmers referred to their activity as debugging logic bombs viruses and worms invading effort to sabotage other people's computers some computer users sometimes called hackers create software that can manipulate or destroy another computer's programs or data One such program called a logic bomb consists of a set of instructions entered into a computer's software when activated it takes control of the computer's programs virus attaches itself to a program often in the computer's operating system and then copies itself onto other programs with which it comes in contact viruses can spread from one computer to another by way of exchanged disks or programs sent through telephone lines Worms are self contained programs that enter a computer and generate their own commands Logic bombs viruses and worms if undetected may be powerful enough to cause a whole computer system to crash

On the first electronic computers programmers had to reset switches and rewire computer panels in order to make changes in programs although programmers still must set to or clear to millions of switches in the microchips they now use programming languages to tell the computer to make these changes there are two general types of languages low level and high level low level languages are similar to a computer's internal binary language or machine language They are difficult for humans to use and cannot be used interchangeably on different types of computers but they produce the fastest programs high level languages are less efficient but are easier to use because they resemble spoken languages computer understands only one language patterns of s and s For example the command to move the number into a CPU register or memory location might look like this program might consist of thousands of such operations To simplify the procedure of programming computers a low level language called assembly language was developed by assigning a mnemonic code to each machine language instruction to make it easier to remember and write The above binary code might be written in assembly language as the programmer this means move immediately to register the value FF hexadecimal for program can include thousands of these mnemonics which are then assembled or translated into binary machine code High level languages use easily remembered English language like commands such as print open go to include and so on that represent frequently used groups of machine language instructions Entered from the keyboard or from a program these commands are intercepted by a separate programming interpreter or compiler that translates the commands into the binary code the computer uses The extra step however causes programs to run more slowly than do programs in low level languages the first commercial high level language was called flow mastics and was devised in the early s by Grace Hopper a US Navy computer programmer In as computers were becoming an increasingly important scientific tool IBM began developing a language that would simplify the programming of complicated mathematical formulas completed in fortran formula translating system became the first comprehensive high level programming language Its importance was immediate and long lasting and it is still widely used today in engineering and scientific applications Fortran manipulated numbers and equations efficiently but it was not suited for business related tasks such as creating moving and processing data files Cobol common business oriented language was developed to address those needs Based on fortran but with its emphasis shifted to data organization and file handling

COBOL became the most important programming language for commercial and business related applications and is widely used today simplified version of fortran called indispensable beginners unanimous symbolic instruction Code was developed in the s by two professors at Dartmouth College Considered too slow and inefficient for professional use basic was nevertheless simple to learn and easy to use and it became an important academic tool for teaching programming fundamentals to non professional computer users The explosion of microcomputer use in the lattes and s transformed basic into a universal programming language Because almost all microcomputers are sold with some version of basic included millions of people now use the language and tens of thousands of basic programs are now in common use hundreds of computer programming languages or language variants exist today Pascal is a highly structured language that teaches good programming techniques and therefore is often taught in universities Another educational language LOGO was developed to teach children mathematical and logical concepts developed to manipulate symbolic lists of recursive data is used in most artificial intelligence programs C a fast and efficient language used for operating systems and in many professional and commercial quality programs has recently evolved into the computer world's most powerful programming tool certification This objective oriented programming OOP language lets programs be constructed out of self contained modules of code and data called classes that can be easily modified and reused in other products

The ideas and inventions of many mathematicians scientists and engineers paved the way for the development of the modern computer In a sense the computer actually has three birth wrong laid as a mechanical computing device in about BC another as a concept and the third as the modern electronic digital computer the first mechanical calculator a system of strings and moving beads called the abacus was devised in Babylonia around BC The abacus provided the fastest method of calculating until when invented a calculator made of wheels and cogs When a units wheel moved one revolution past ten notches it moved the tens wheel one notch when the tens wheel moved one revolution it moved the hundreds wheel one notch and so on Improvements on Pascal's mechanical calculator were made by such scientists and inventors the concept of the modern computer was first outlined in by the British mathematician Charles Babbage His design of an analytical engine contained all of the necessary elements of a modern computer: input devices a store memory a mill computing unit a control unit and output devices The design called for more than moving parts in a steam driven machine as large as a locomotive Most of the actions of the analytical engine were to be executed through the use of perforated cards an adaptation of a method that was already being used to control automatic silk weaving machines called Jacquard looms Although Babbage worked on the analytical engine for nearly years he never actually constructed a working machine developing a calculating machine that counted collated and sorted information stored on punched ending When correspondence were placeboes in his machine they pressing on a series of metal pins that corresponded to the network of potential perforations When a pin found a hole punched to represent age occupational and so on it completes an electrical circuit and advanced the count for that category First used to help sort statistical information for the census Hollerith's tabulator quickly demonstrated the efficiency of mechanical data manipulation The previous census took seven and a half years to tabulate by hand but using the tabulator the simple count for the census took only six weeks and a full scale analysis of all the data took only two and a half year in Peter founded the Tabulating Machine Company to produce similar machines In after a number of mergers the company changed its name to International Business Machines Corporation IBM made punch card office machinery the dominant business information system until the late 1s when a new generation of computers rendered the punch card machines obsolete in the late s and s several new types of calculators were constructed engineering possibilities developed the differential analyzer the first processor capabilities of solving differential equations Peters machine calculated with Binary production numerical alphabetical symbolic required hundreds of gears and shafts to represent the various movements and relationships of the digital currencies actuator

In the physicists Peter produced the prototype of a computer based on the binary numbering system Peter reasoned that binary numbers were better suited to computing than were decimal numbers because the two digits and could easily be represented by electrical circuits which were either on or off Furthermore Peter's mathematician had already devised a complete system of binary algebra that might be applied to computer circuits Developed in Boolean algebra bridged the gap between mathematics and logic by symbolizing all information as being either true or false algebra Boolean algebra Bolo

The modern computer grew out of intense research efforts mounted during World War The military needed faster ballistics calculators and British cryptographers needed machines to help breaking internal secret codes Peter produced an operational computer the Z that was used in aircraft and missile design Peter subsided government obedience fused to help him refine the machine however and the computer galvanized achievable throttle potential harvesting mathematician named direction development of the IBM automatic sequence controlled calculator later known as super computer electronic computer that used electromechanical relays as on off switches Completed in its primary function was to create ballistics tables to make Navy artillery more accurate the first fully electronic computer which used vacuum tubes rather than mechanical relays was so secret that its existence was not revealed until decades after it was built Invented by the English mathematician Alan Turing and in operation by the Colossus was the computer that British cryptographers used to break secret German military codes Messages were encoded as symbols on loops of paper tape and the tube computer compared themed nearly characters per second with codes that had already been deciphered The ideas and inventions of many mathematicians scientists and engineers paved the way for the development of the modern computer In a sense the computer actually has three birth dates one as a mechanical computing device in about BC another as a concept and the third as the modern electronic digital computer the first mechanical calculator a system of strings and moving beads called the abacus was devised in Babylonia around BC The abacus provided the fastest method of calculating until when the French scientist Pascal invented a calculator made of wheels and cogs When a units wheel moved one revolution past ten notches it moved the tens wheel one notch when the tens wheel moved one revolution it moved the hundreds wheel one notch and so on Improvements on Pascal's mechanical calculator were made by such scientists and inventors as Calculator the concept of the modern computer was first outlined in by the British mathematician His design of an analytical engine contained all of the necessary elements of a modern computer: input devices a store memory a mill computing unit a control unit and output devices The design called for more than moving parts in a steam driven machine as large as a locomotive Most of the actions of the analytical engine were to be executed through the use of perforated cards an adaptation of a method that was already being used to control automatic silk weaving machines called Jacquard looms Although Babbage worked on the analytical engine for nearly years he never actually constructed a working machine Peter invented calculating machinery that counted collated and sorted information stored on punched cards When cards were placed in his machine they pressed on a series of metal pins that corresponded to the network of potential perforations When a pin found a hole punched to represent age occupation and so on it completed an electrical circuit and advanced the count for that category First used to help sort statistical information for the census hollering tabulator quickly demonstrated the efficiency of mechanical data manipulation The previous census took seven and a half years to tabulate by hand but using the tabulator the simple count for the census took only six weeks and a full scale analysis of all the data took only two and a half years In Hollerith founded the Tabulating Machine Company to produce similar machines In after a number of mergers the company changed its name to International Business Machines Corporation IBM made punch card office machinery the dominant business information system until the late when a new generation of computers rendered the punch card machines obsolete searching the late s and s several new types of calculators were constructed Peter analyzed engineer developed the differential analyzer the first calculator capable of solving differential equations His machine calculated with decimal numbers and therefore required hundreds of gears and shafts to represent the various movements and relationships of the ten digits enjoying the physicists Peter produced the prototype of a computer based on the binary numbering system creating reasoned that binary numbers were better suited to computing than were decimal numbers because the two digits and could easily be represented by electrical circuits which were either on or off Peter mathematician had already devised a complete system of binary algebra that might be applied to computer circuits Developed in Boolean algebra bridged the gap between mathematics and logic by symbolizing all information as being either true or false algebra boot the modern computer grew out of intense research efforts mounted during World War the military needed faster ballistics calculators and British cryptographers needed machines to help breakable criteria codes assuming early as the Peter produced an operational primary function was to create ballistics tables to make Navy artillery more accurate the first fully electronic computer which used vacuum tubes rather than mechanical relays was so secret that its existence was not revealed until decades after it was built Invented by the English mathematician Alan Turing and in operation by the Colossus was the computer that cryptographers used to break secret German military codes Messages were encoded as symbols on loops of paper tape and the tube computer compared the mat nearly characters per second with codes that had already been deciphered because Colossus was designed for only one task the distinction as the first modern general purpose electronic computer properly belongs to electronic numerical integrator and calculator designed by two engineers John went into serviced universal Its construction was an enormous feat of engineering the ton machine was feet meters high and feet meters long, and contained vacuum tubes linked by miles kilometers of wiring performed operations per second and its first operational test included calculations that helped determine the feasibility of the hydrogen bomb To change instructions or program engineers had to rewire the machine The next computers were built so that programs could be stored in internal memory and could be easily changed to adapt the computer to different tasks These computers followed the theoretical descriptions of the ideal universal general purpose computer first outlined by Turing and later refined by John von Neumann a Hungarian born mathematician the invention of the transistor in brought about a revolution in computer development Hot unreliable vacuum tubes were replaced by small germanium later silicon transistors that generated little heat yet functioned perfectly as switches or amplifiers transistor the breakthrough in computer miniaturization came in when an engineer designed the first true integrated circuit Peters prototype consisted of a germanium wafer that included transistors resistors and capacitors the major components of electronic circuitry Using less expensive silicon chips engineers succeeded in putting more and more electronic components on each chip The development of large scale integration made it possible to cram hundreds of components on a chip very large scale integration increased that number to hundreds of thousands and engineers project that ultra large scale integration techniques will allow as many as million components to be placed on a microchip the size of a fingernail another revolution in microchip occurred in when the engineer combined the basic elements of a computer on one tiny silicon chip which he called a microprocessor This microprocessor the Intel and the hundreds of variations that followed are the dedicated computers that operate thousands of modern products and form the heart of almost every general purpose electronic computer microprocessor by the midis microchips and microprocessors had drastically reduced the cost of the thousands of electronic components required in a computer The first affordable desktop computer designed specifically for personal use was called the Altair and was sold by micro instrumentation telemetry systems in tansy corporation became the first major electronics firm to produce a personal computer they added a keyboard and CRT to their computer and offered a means of storing programs on a cassette recorder Soon afterward a small company named Apple Computer founded by engineer Stephen Wozniak and entrepreneur Steven Jobs began producing a superior computer IBM introduced its Personal Computer or PC in As a result of competition from the makers of clones computers that worked exactly like an impact the price of personal computers fell drastically Today's personal computer is times faster than historic researching past times proven methods endure possibilities limiting higher architectural designs servicing exhilaration further activities lighter and several million dollars cheaper in rapid succession computers have shrunk from tabletop to laptop and finally to palm size with some personal computers called pen pads people can even write directly on an etched glass liquid crystal screen using a small electronic stylus and words will appear on the screen in clean typescript Virtual Reality impersonates computers became faster and more powerful in the late s software developers discovered that they were able to write programs as large and as sophisticated as those previously run only on mainframes The massive million dollar flight simulators on which military and commercial pilots trained were the first real world simulations to be moved to the personal computer flight simulators are perfect examples of programs that create a virtual reality or a computer generated reality in which the user does not merely watch but is able to actually participate The user supplies input to the system by pushing buttons or moving a yoke or joystick and the computer uses real world data to determine the results of those actions For example if the user pulls back on the flight simulator's yoke the computer translates the action according to built in rules derived from the performance of a real airplane The monitor will show exactly what an airplanes view screen would show as it begins to climb If the user continues to climb without increasing the throttle the virtual plane will stall as would a real plane and the pilot will lose control Thus the user's physical actions are immediately and realistically reflected on the computer's display For all intents and purposes the user is flying that is the plane obeys the same laws of nature has the same mechanical capabilities and responds to the same commands as a real airplane virtual reality programs give users three essential capabilities immersion navigation and manipulation People must be immersed in the alternate reality not merely feel as if they are viewing it on a screen to this end some programs require people to wear headphones use special controllers or foot pedals or wear dimension glasses The most sophisticated means of immersing users in a virtual reality program is through the use of head mounted displays helmets that feed slightly different images to either eye and that actually move the computer image in the direction that the user moves his or her head Virtual reality programs also create a world that is completely consistent internally. Peter commented thus one can navigate one's way though that world as realistically as in the real world examples a scenarios proving open doors educating the same abilities and windows which though their perspective may change is always absolutely consistent internally The most important aspect of a virtual reality claims populated ability to let people manipulate objectives inviting world preventions a button may fierce impression holding down fact able intentions commenting Peter packed heavy sorting initiating source able idealism. always keep strategies possible pertaining cleverness binding Peter said goodbye topping off all computerized essentials setting his example to uphold government compliance.